NO LIMITS

A Kingdom Perspective on Making Disciples

Viv Penfold

"Of the increase of His government and peace there will be no end."
Isaiah

"Go therefore and make disciples of all the nations."
Jesus Christ

First Published in Great Britain in 2016 by

Ohm Books
68 Brackenwood Drive
Leeds
LS8 1RJ, UK

A CIP catalogue record for this book is available from the British Library

ISBN 978-0-9931064-1-5

For More Information on No Limits Ministries, please visit www.nolimitsmission.co.uk

Dedicated to the memory of
D.B. ABRAHAM
(1947-2004)

or as I knew him,

My friend

We were jokingly known as twins (same 'Father' different mothers). You were a loyal servant of Christ and a genuine discipler. Visionary, dynamic church planter, partner in the gospel, and yet a humble man, a great adventurer, and an indomitable spirit.

This book is also dedicated to Rani Elizabeth, his life and ministry partner, and all the disciples, pastors, and church planters throughout Andhra Pradesh, India who have proceeded from their ministry.

CONTENTS

PART THREE: PRACTICAL DISCIPLEMAKING AND PERSONAL EXPERIENCES

Introduction

My Journey

Do you believe that God speaks to you? I do. At the time, I had been a Christ-follower for almost 30 years and, to use a misleading term, in 'full-time' ministry for well over 25 of those years. By the grace of God, my wife and I had planted and pastored churches, re-purposed others, been involved in missions both at home and abroad, and I had served as the Regional Church Planting Director for our denomination and, later, as the Regional Superintendent.

Recently, as I sat in my study at home, I contemplated the future. I had passed on the baton of leadership of our current church and was no longer required to serve the denomination in the capacity of Regional leader due to structural re-organisation. What next, if anything? At the age of 62 and feeling the effects of constant ministry, I began to wonder if it was time to buy a greenhouse and grow tomatoes!

Suddenly, the thought came to me (and I believe it was the Holy Spirit speaking) in the form of a question: "Can you believe me for a thousand new churches in the next ten years?" Panicking, I searched my heart for a response, but I could only come up with the answer Ezekiel gave the Lord when asked "Can these dry bones live?" My safe reply was, "You alone know, Lord".

As I meditated upon these things, I began to think of all the money we had spent over the years planting churches here in the UK, as well as in Andhra Pradesh, India in partnership with my good friend D.B. Abraham of New Life Fellowship. Taking into account the Bible College and Ministry Training Centres for leadership training, buildings, facilities, support of workers, literature, transportation and equipment, I soon realised that we would need something in excess of the U.S. defence budget to accomplish a thousand new churches using the same methods we have previously employed. In view of this, I drew the conclusion that the Lord would have to show us a different strategy if we were to even begin contemplating such a task.

I became preoccupied with these things. Every waking moment was consumed with thinking and praying for guidance. Within two weeks, I felt the Lord had spoken - and in a quite unusual way. I was reading the book 'Radical' by American pastor David Platt when I came across an anecdote about a conversation the author had with a young Sudanese man named Bullen.

"We discussed what God was doing in each of our lives, and we talked about the plans God had for us in the future. In the middle of that conversation, Bullen lowered the cup of hot tea from his lips, looked me in the eyes, and said:

"David, I am going to impact the world."

An interesting statement. Here was a guy in the African bush with almost no resources. A guy who hadn't seen much of the world beyond the villages that surrounded him. A guy who, by all outward appearances, did not have much hope of changing his lot in life.

"Bullen, how are you going to impact the world?" I asked.

"I'm going to make disciples of all nations," he said.

"So, you are going to impact the world by making disciples of all nations?"

That grin immediately spread across his face.

"Why not?" he asked. Then he went back to sipping his tea.

I'll never forget those two words.

Why not?

As I read the book, God spoke. Nothing new, I guess, but in that moment everything seemed to drop into place. So many things that I had been learning over the past few years all of a sudden made a lot more sense. Fundamentally, that is what this book is about. As Luke writes to Theophilus in Luke 1:3:

"…it seemed good to me also…to write an orderly account."

I wish I could say as Luke does in the same verse, *"having had perfect understanding of all things from the very first"*, but it wouldn't be true. However, I do now believe I have a few insights that I think are worth passing on.

I truly believe that a restoration of biblical discipleship is what the Spirit is saying to the church in these days and so, here we go . . . .

Foreword

The Centrality of Disciple-Making

I suppose it might seem strange that, in a book about making disciples, I want to talk about other things first. However, it is these very things that will help us to understand the reason for and the importance of making disciples. These things include the Kingdom of God; His Eternal Purpose; and how, through Fruitfulness, Multiplication and Dominion, God will get what He wants. In order to really understand the Great Commission we have to understand something of God's 'Big Picture'.

I was travelling in India with a friend of mine, Bruce Millar, and I was challenged by some of his teaching. He started off by saying that many people's understanding has been defined by a lot of badly informed preaching and teaching. So many people, he explained, believe that Jesus came to save them from their sins and take them to heaven when they die. "No", he said, "In 2 Peter 3:13, the apostle says that, in keeping with God's promise, we are looking forward to a new heaven and a new earth, where righteousness is at home". Verse 14 says that we are to look forward to these things, although verse 16 says that some things are "hard to understand."

There are two things I wish I'd understood when I was a new believer which would have helped me interpret the Scriptures more accurately: Firstly, not only was Jesus a Jew (he was a rabbi sent to the lost sheep of Israel), but also that the Bible is a Jewish book. It's a bit like buttoning up your shirt - if you don't start with the right button in the right buttonhole, then you won't get the right end product. The second thing I wish I'd understood was the 'Big Picture'. This is a bit like attempting a 1,000 piece jigsaw - often the only way you know where your little piece fits, is by looking at the picture on the lid of the box. We could call it perspective, or a strategic view.

The Church is to be a sign and a wonder: A shop window to the world to allow them to see into the Kingdom of God. A sign points to something and a wonder…well, it makes you wonder! Shop windows must grab attention if they are to invite the sales resistant inside to see more. But how is the church to be a sign and a wonder? In order to answer this, we need to go right back to the beginning. We need to look at the 'Big Picture' in order to see where our little piece of the jigsaw fits into the whole. In short, we need to gain overall perspective.

Bruce Millar went on to explain this 'Big Picture' like a five act play:

Act 1: Creation & Fall

Act 2: Abraham and God's dealings with him to further His purposes through the nation of Israel. God's problem was how to put the world right through a flawed people.

Act 3: God's solution, Jesus! God re-inaugurates his Kingdom on earth through the resurrection of Christ.

Act 4: Pentecost to Christ's 2nd coming (Age of the Kingdom);

Act 5: What takes place for eternity . . . on earth (2 Pet.3:13).

Bruce explained that we are currently living in Act 4, the in-between time of 'now' and 'not yet'. We are 'in training for reigning'. We are still only heirs (Romans 8:17), but we are predestined to be conformed to the image of His Son (Romans 8:29) and predestined to be adopted as sons (Ephesians 1:5). This is where discipleship comes in! I will explain this more fully later under the section about the Good News of the Kingdom.

One of the main tasks of the apostles was to ensure that the churches were holding fast to the true gospel that had been delivered to them - the gospel (good news) of the Kingdom. Unfortunately, I believe that we have strayed to false gospels (Galatians 1:6) which promise things that they can't deliver. Only the Gospel of the Kingdom "*...is the power of God for salvation to everyone who believes*" (Rom. 1:16). I believe we have made it about other things, such as:

- Eternal fire insurance (safety, a destination)

- Living forever (eternal life)
- Making church members (an organisation and following rules)
- Getting decisions (getting people to accept/ receive Jesus as an 'end point')

Actually, the Gospel is about making disciples. King Jesus does not want fans: He wants followers; and not just followers, but also learners who understand what he wants. I know that we are saved by grace through faith, not by works, but I believe we disciple people to salvation (learn, believe and obey) and that is what this book is really about.

The big issue is that, as with any kingdom, King Jesus requires total allegiance and complete obedience. Therefore, the key to entrance into the Kingdom of God is repentance. Jesus said, "Repent for the kingdom is here!" Something has to take place: – something has to change. We have been told that we must repent of our sins, and that is of course very true. However, there is something much deeper than that. We must also repent of ourselves!

Some years ago on a rooftop in Hyderabad, India, I believe that God spoke to me in a special way. It was both a revelation and a personal call to repentance. The question came to me as a thought:

"What is wrong with my church?"

I replied: "Lord, I believe it is a lack of authentic discipleship".

The voice in my heart and mind came back: "That is

not the problem. The problem is that my people worship false gods!"

I spoke out loud: "No, Lord, we worship You, the One True and Living God; the God of Abraham, Isaac and Jacob".

The Lord then said: "Many of my people create Me in their own image (what they want me to be like) and the result is that they end up worshipping themselves".

I was left not only agreeing with God, but also under deep conviction that I had also been guilty of this and needed to repent of this sin.

The big issue that we all have to get to grips with is the issue of 'LORDSHIP'. We have to settle in our hearts and minds who will be the practical, functional Lord of our lives. We cannot be true disciples of Jesus Christ and insist on our own lordship. Jesus said that unless we deny self, take up our cross and follow Him, we cannot be His disciples. So, in this first part, let me start the big picture by looking at the Kingdom of God, which is also often referred to as the Kingdom of Heaven. Please note that the Kingdom of Heaven is not a geographical place, but is the realm or sphere of God. It is the rule, reign, authority and dominion of the King.

PART ONE: CONTEXT

Chapter 1: Kingdom Origins

One of the best books that I have read on this subject is 'Rediscovering the Kingdom' by Myles Munro and I want to acknowledge it as a major influence in writing this first part.

As we read the Bible carefully, we will notice that the central theme that runs throughout is that of the Kingdom of God. God existed before all things and began his creative process by first producing the entire invisible world. This act of creation initiated the concept of 'ruler' and 'rulership'. An-other word for ruler is 'king', and this is the word the Bible uses. Furthermore, a king assumes a kingdom. So, God has a Kingdom. Since God IS love, his actions would naturally be motivated by that characteristic, and one of the obvious qualities of love is that it has to give and share. It is from this motivation that God created the world - the visible aspect of his Kingdom, - and, of course, mankind; whom He created in his own image and likeness. An important task that we need to undertake is discovering the origin and purpose of man.

Matthew 13:44 says that the Kingdom of Heaven is like treasure hidden in a field. So many of us are in the field but are completely unaware of the treasure that is in the field with us. That is why we don't go and 'sell everything' in order to buy it. So many people have spent their lives searching for the ideal – ideologies carry a variety of labels. Yet, no matter how hard man has tried to re-create his own world, the fulfilment of man's hope and desire for utopia still eludes him. I think the source of this desire is God himself as He leads us to seek Him. God created us in his image to be fruitful, multiply and have dominion over our environment. No matter how far man thinks he has progressed, the ability to achieve dominion and power over life and death on Earth still eludes him.

Man is possessed by a desire to dominate, rule and control his personal private world and his environment. He is in search of the ultimate governing power of dominion. The desire for power is inherent in the human spirit, although it is not power, but authority that we really need. To understand this desire for power, however, it is necessary to understand the original purpose and design of mankind and the assignment for which he was created.

The book of Genesis opens with God's activity in the creation of the physical world. Since God is spirit, his intention was to establish his Kingdom in that physical world without having to come visibly into that world himself. The purpose of the invisible God would be served by a visible, physical creation that was the result of his creative genius. His plan would be carried out by creating from His own spirit being a family who would be just like him, created in his exact image. As his representatives, they would release, establish, and implement his invisible Kingdom in the physical world. God created the Garden of Eden as an example of his design and gave man the task of making the rest of the planet like it. This was his original purpose for creating mankind and it hasn't changed! From the very beginning, God's plan for mankind centred on the fact that God desired to have a personal relationship with man and vice versa, and that within this context mankind would be his vice-regents or ambassadors. It was never God's plan to establish a religion. Religion is the result of man's response to a deep spiritual vacuum in the recesses of his soul, which is the result of 'the Fall'.

Genesis 1:26-28 New International Version (NIV):

26 *Then God said, "Let us make mankind in our image, in our likeness, so that they may rule over the fish in the sea and the birds in the sky, over the livestock and all the wild animals, and over all the creatures that move along the ground."*
27 *So God created mankind in His own image, in the image of God He created them; male and female He created them.*
28 *God blessed them and said to them, "Be fruitful and increase in number; fill the earth and subdue it. Rule over the fish in the sea and the birds in the sky and over every living creature that moves on the ground."*

When we read the verses above, there are a number of principles in this first mission statement:

- Man was made in God's image – In the original Hebrew the words *'tselem'* and *'demut'* are used, both meaning essential nature, copy, characteristics and essence. So, man was to be a spirit being as an expression of God's moral and spiritual nature. These attributes made him 'god-like'.
- God created man. This does not refer to gender but was the name given by the Creator for the species of spirits that came out of his spirit. Man is plural, and non-gender specific in this context.
- The Creator said "let them have dominion over the Earth". This is the transfer of power and authority from God to man, from Heaven to Earth, and from the unseen to the seen world. He did not say let "us" have dominion.
- Let them have dominion. The word 'dominion' lays the foundation for the Kingdom concept as it relates to God's purpose and plan for the human species.
- "Over the fish of the sea, the birds of the air, the livestock, earth, and all that creep on the ground". It is essential to note that the man was not given dominion over his fellow man.

So, what is dominion? The Hebrew words '*mashal*', '*mamlakah*' and '*malkut*' are used. The Greek derivative is the word '*basileia*'. These words, to describe 'dominion', include the concepts of 'rule', 'sovereignty', 'to reign', 'to master', 'to be king', 'royal rule', and 'kingly'. Thus, the definition of 'dominion' can be crafted from all these words in the following way:

To be given dominion means to be established as a sovereign, kingly ruler, master or governor, responsible for reigning over a designated territory. Such a person would have the inherent authority to represent the territory, resources, and all that constitutes that kingdom. The fact that such dominion is given presupposes someone of higher authority who bestows that dominion.

According to Genesis 1:26, Man (male and female) were to have dominion over the Earth. They were to exercise their royal sovereignty as a 'corporate kingship'. Therefore, all mankind (male and female) were created rulers and kings. Mankind is a kingdom of kings, and that is why Jesus is known as the 'King of kings'.

The original and ultimate goal of God the Creator was to colonise the Earth with Heaven and establish it as a visible territory of his invisible world. His purpose was to have His will done and the heavenly kingdom come on Earth just as it is in Heaven.

Let's just reconsider Genesis 1:26-28 and its implications as to what man's original rulership did and did not involve:

- God gave man dominion over earth.
- God gave man dominion over creation and earth, not other men.
- God didn't give man dominion over heaven.

- God didn't give man a religion, but a relationship.
- God didn't promise man heaven, but earth.

The Bible says that we are ambassadors of Heaven (Eph. 6:20; 2 Cor. 5:20). An ambassadorial representative is only as viable and legal as his relationship with his government. For this reason, the most important relationship the first man, Adam, had on Earth was with Heaven. This is why the Holy Spirit of God was intimate with mankind from the beginning. This relationship made the Holy Spirit of God the most important person on earth and established him as the key component of the Kingdom of Heaven on Earth. So, we see that the encounter of mankind with the devil in Genesis 3 was designed to drive man from the Garden and from his relationship with God and Heaven, resulting in the loss of the Kingdom of Heaven on Earth.

What happened was an 'act of treason' - a crime that carries the death penalty! Adam and his descendants committed the ultimate act of betrayal, deserving the penalty of death. When Adam fell through this act of treason, not only did he lose his personal relationship with his heavenly Father, but he also lost a kingdom. The Fall also resulted in the loss of relationship with the Earth and with other men. Adam became an 'ambassador without portfolio'.

However, Adam did not lose Heaven when he fell; rather, he lost Earth and dominion over it. This is what God meant in Genesis 2:7 when He said "you will surely die" - Man's spiritual disconnection from his source and kingdom resulted in:

- Loss of position and disposition
- Self-consciousness and shame
- Fear and intimidation of authority
- Loss of dominion over nature/ the Earth
- Frustrated toil and hatred of labour
- Pain and discomfort; and the need for human accountability e.g. governments, police etc.

Fortunately, God had a response: He promised to restore all that was lost in the Garden. At the heart of this promise is the coming of a 'seed', an 'offspring' who would break the power of the adversary over mankind and regain the authority and dominion Adam once held. This was the first promise of a messiah-king and the return of the Kingdom.

Genesis 3:14-15 records God's response to this treason:

14 *So the Lord God said to the serpent, "Because you have done this, "Cursed are you above all livestock and all wild animals! You will crawl on your belly and you will eat dust all the days of your life.*
15 *And I will put enmity between you and the woman, and between your offspring and hers; he will crush your head, and you will strike his heel."*

Only the Kingdom of Heaven on Earth can solve man's eternal problem. I truly believe that religion preoccupies us to distract us from our hunger and emptiness for the Kingdom. In essence, religion is designed to keep us too busy to fill our assignment for the Kingdom. Religion is hard work. We will never rest until we find the Kingdom. Religion is the toil of mankind in his search for the King-dom. However, God's original purpose and plan for His creation was to:

- Establish a family of sons, not servants.
- Establish a kingdom, not a religious organisation.
- Establish a kingdom of son-kings, not subjects.
- Establish a commonwealth of citizens, not religious members.
- Establish relationship with man, not a religion.
- Extend His heavenly government to earth.
- Influence earth from heaven through mankind.

Chapters 21 and 22 of the book of Revelation are the eternal fulfilment of God's original plan as outlined in Genesis 1 and 2. This is the true Gospel of the Kingdom - the Gospel according to Jesus, not the Gospel about Jesus. It is not just a Gospel of Salvation, but the Gospel of salvage of an entire creation. However, what we must not lose sight of is the 'now' and the 'not yet' aspects of the Kingdom. We are not currently ruling, but we are undergoing 'training for reigning'. Basically, that is what discipleship is all about - learning to think, speak and act like the King.

John 8:31-35 says that "a slave has no permanent place in the family", but sons, on the other hand, are part of the family: They are heirs who will inherit everything that belongs to their father. We are destined to be sons, not subjects. God does not want to rule us, but to have a family that shares His rulership. God's Kingdom is different from earthly kingdoms in that it has no subjects. There are no peasants in the Kingdom of God, only sons - everyone is related to the King.

God intends Man to become kingdom citizens, not Christians. The Lord never intended that those who believe in Jesus as Messiah and King would be referred to as Christians. The word Christian has too much baggage with it, it refers to a whole host of people, some of them having no connection to the Kingdom. Too many Christians are simply religious people, but citizens of the Kingdom are a legal people - legal in the sense that, by virtue of a spiritual birth, each individual in the Kingdom has the rights, privileges, responsibilities and blessings of citizens of this heavenly Kingdom. We must be delivered from our religious mindsets and have our thinking readjusted so that we can take on a regal (kingdom) mindset.
Citizenship is always considered a privilege, usually reserved for those born into that nation or kingdom. There may be other ways of obtaining citizenship, but birthright is the guaranteed form of 'son-ship' and the resulting rights of citizenship.

Now, God requires a physical body to get His will done on Earth. Through Jesus, He got that body and now, through the indwelling of Christ in us, he can continue that work. One important key to this is the power of prayer; for by the power of prayer we can arrange to get God's power into our earthly realm. Prayer is important because it is our means of constantly entreating God to 'interfere' in the affairs of men on Earth. In Matthew 6:10, Jesus taught his disciples to pray, *"Your Kingdom come, Your will be done on earth as it is in heaven"*. St. Augustine said, "Without God we cannot, without us God will not".

When we pray we are communicating with a divine government for whom we are ambassadors. We must build a Kingdom mentality as we train for reigning. We are children of the King and so his Kingdom belongs to us as well! In Luke 12:32 Jesus said, *"Do not be afraid, little flock, for your Father has been pleased to give you the kingdom"*. We must conduct ourselves in a manner worthy of this privilege as wise children giving careful and confident management of a realm that we stand to inherit one day.

In Genesis chapter 3, the rulers became the ruled and our problem is that too often we just settle for the contract that the prodigal son wanted - to be a servant in his father's house. In John 15:15 Jesus said, *"I no longer call you servants, because a servant does not know his master's business. In-stead, I have called you friends, for everything that I learned from my Father I have made known to you".* Jesus Christ is our saviour by circumstance, but He is our elder brother by a natural/ spiritual genealogy. Hebrews 2:11 says, *"Both the One who makes men holy and those who are made holy are of the same family. So Jesus is not ashamed to call them brothers".*

So often, however, we tend to relate to him as our saviour much more than as our big brother. The truth is that it only takes a moment to believe in Jesus, but it takes a lifetime to learn how to think, speak and act like the children of God. We need a change of mind (repentance) – we must learn to think and act (faith) like kings again, to lay hold of the spirit and attitude of kings.

Chapter 2: Enter the King and the Kingdom

As we have seen, the message of the Bible is primarily and obviously about a Kingdom. If we don't understand the principles of kingdom, it is impossible for us to fully understand the Bible and its message. We have muddied the water by converting the message of the Kingdom of God into a moral belief system. We have made the gospel about forgiveness of 'sins' and going to heaven when we die. The result is that religion has become an end in itself, distinguishing itself from the Kingdom concept with pride. The fact is that Jesus came to earth to restore what Adam lost and accomplish what the nation of Israel failed to do. He brought a Kingdom message. Adam lost a kingdom, not a religion. Conversely, Jesus came to restore a kingdom, not a religion.

Whenever a sovereign is to arrive, it is announced and preparations are made far in advance. Even the people have to be prepared. This was the role of John the Baptist. John's message was not about religion, but the arrival of the Kingdom of Heaven. Jesus stated that John was the greatest of all the prophets that ever lived (Matt 11:11).

Jesus' priesthood was his redemptive function, but to be King was his eternal disposition and destiny (Jn. 18:37, 19:12, Lk. 4:43). One of the most important discoveries in life is the discovery of purpose and Jesus' mission was his purpose. Yes,

He came to die for our sins and make a way for us to enter the Kingdom of God, but His main purpose was to complete Israel's story and restore the Kingdom and proclaim it. Matt. 4:17 says *"From that time on Jesus began to preach, "Repent, for the kingdom of heaven is near"."* Some versions translate the word 'near' as 'at hand' or 'has arrived'. In other words, his first declaration was the introduction and arrival of a kingdom, not a religion (Matt. 10:7, 12:28, 18:23, 24:14, Lk. 4:43-44, 8:1a, 9:11, 12:31, 12:32, 16:16-17, 18:17, 22:29, Jn. 18:36-37). These are just a few of the declarations made by Jesus concerning his mission, purpose, and message; and it is obvious that his intent was to declare, establish, and invite all men to enter the Kingdom of God.

This is in direct contrast with the focus of religious activity and religion's preoccupation with going to heaven. Matthew 5:5 says, *"Blessed are the meek, for they will inherit the earth"*. In Matthew 12:28 Jesus says, *"But if I drive out demons by the Spirit of God, then the Kingdom of God has come up-on you"*. This verse seems to indicate the return of the dominion power that Adam lost in his disobedience – a re-connection of Earth with Heaven. To all who believed in and followed him, Jesus restored their citizenship rights in the Kingdom of Heaven. Luke 22:29, *"And I confer on you a kingdom, just as my Father conferred one on me"*. This is the position of an ambassador, not a religious designation, but a governmental one. In 2 Corinthians 5:20 Paul writes, *"We are therefore Christ's ambassadors, as though God were making His appeal through us. We implore you on Christ's be-half: Be reconciled to God"*.

We need to develop and maintain a Kingdom mindset. The first thing Jesus said in order for some-one to come into the kingdom was "repent". We need to change our minds, to change our thinking and mindset. From now on, only one opinion matters - the King's. There is no vote in the Kingdom of God; His word is supreme and absolute! Jesus is the King, not the president. We did not vote Him in, and we cannot vote Him out. We need to lay aside our democratic mindset and start thinking like Kingdom citizens and ambassadors.

Part of healthy Kingdom thinking is to have a clear and proper understanding of what scripture says concerning the End Times. A Biblical understanding of the "appearing of Christ" and other apocalyptic themes is something that very few people have. The important thing is that *"this gospel of the Kingdom will be preached in the whole world as a testimony to all nations, and then the end will come"* (Matt 24:14). This verse suggests that the specific hour of Christ's appearing is in God's hands, but the general timing of it is in ours! (See also 2 Peter 3:12 – *"looking for and hastening the coming of the day of the Lord"*).

In the meantime, we are to be busy making disciples and proclaiming the Gospel of the Kingdom. If Jesus has not yet 'appeared', it is because our commission to preach the Gospel of the Kingdom and make disciples of all nations has not been fulfilled. How many churches today are actively and conscientiously preaching the gospel of the Kingdom? We preach prosperity, we preach healing, we preach faith, we preach deliverance, we preach gifts, we especially preach salvation, but how many preach the Kingdom of God?

Why do we have so many Muslims, Hindus, Buddhists, animists and atheists futilely searching for God? Is it because the church hasn't done its job. The possibility of their salvation is contained in the Kingdom message - the good news of the Kingdom!

Matthew 9: 35-38:

"Jesus went through all the towns and villages, teaching in their synagogues, proclaiming the good news of the kingdom and healing every disease and sickness. When he saw the crowds, he had compassion on them, because they were harassed and helpless, like sheep without a shepherd. Then he said to his disciples, "The harvest is plentiful but the workers are few. Ask the Lord of the harvest, therefore, to send out workers into his harvest field.""

Where are the workers? Jesus said the harvest is plentiful but the labourers are few. He was talking not only about the quantity of workers but the quality of them as well. The problem, as I see it, is twofold: Many believers who should be working in the harvest are not, and many who are working are not doing a very good job. Mark 3:14 says, *"He appointed twelve . . . that they might be with him, and that he might send them out to preach"*. Many people who come into the church get 'saved' because they want 'eternal fire insurance'. They want to make sure they don't go to hell. That's one of the reasons we see so many backsliders and spiritual dropouts. Someone gets afraid of the fire and comes to a meeting where a preacher tells him how to avoid hell by turning to Christ. Out of fear, he runs to the front of the church, confesses his sins, accepts Jesus, gets his 'fire insurance policy' and calls it salvation.

After a couple of months, he eventually becomes bored, frustrated and depressed with this new 'religion' thing and ends up going back into the world. Why? Be-cause the world promises (although it doesn't deliver) the very thing he expected to find in the church but the church failed to deliver: Power for living. The Kingdom of God is all about power, but many believers and others miss it because few churches truly teach it.

People everywhere are looking for the Kingdom, even if they don't recognise it by that name. In the Bible, for instance, Nicodemus came to Jesus in John 3:3 and the Lord told him he needed to be 'born again'. A rich young ruler came seeking the Kingdom and asked, *"What must I do to inherit eternal life?"* Jesus told him to sell all and give to the poor and follow him (Mk. 10:21). In John 4, a Samaritan woman asked Jesus to *"give me this water"*. In other words they were asking, "How do I get into this Kingdom?" It is exactly the same today. People are looking for the Kingdom. That is why the harvest is ready. All over the world, Muslims are getting saved. Why? Because people are not looking for religion;

they are looking for power to live life to the full, and the Kingdom offers that power. The Kingdom represents the dominion we lost when Adam and Eve fell, and our nature drives us forward in a constant attempt to restore it (most often in the wrong way). Of course there is still a major difference between this 'present evil age' and the 'age to come', but nevertheless, the harvest is ready and if we preach the gospel of the Kingdom of God, people will respond.

In Matthew 22:21 Jesus said, *"Render unto Caesar that which is Caesar's and render unto God that which is God's."* He was simply saying that we should give each kingdom its due. If Caesar asks for money, we should give it because paying taxes is one responsibility of citizens of a free country, but if he asks for our first allegiance, that is where we draw the line. This principle was demonstrated by the three Hebrew boys Shadrach, Meschach and Abednego, who refused to worship anyone but the Living God. We see that in matters of the Spirit, God demands and deserves total, undivided allegiance.

Chapter 3: The Good News of the Kingdom

The word 'gospel' means 'good news'. The good news about the Kingdom of God must be our prime concern. The driving motivation of Jesus' life was not to get us to heaven – that is the goal of religion - but to get us into the Kingdom. In other words, to get Heaven to Earth. We must remember that God does not need to conquer the Earth because it already belongs to Him (Psalm 24:1). The Kingdom of God is after the world of human hearts and minds. Our Kingdom is not from this world, but it is for this world. However, sin has blinded our eyes regarding who we are and where we came from. God plans to restore everything that was lost in the Garden of Eden - a place of honour, relationship, dominion, and authority. He wants us to rediscover and reclaim our inheritance with the result that the kingdoms of this world become the Kingdom of our God and the "*Earth is filled with the knowledge of the glory of the Lord as the waters cover the sea*" (Hab. 2:14).

The Bible talks about us receiving the 'spirit of adoption' (Rom. 8:15, 23; 9:4; Gal. 4:5; Eph. 1:5). This is not like our western use of the term 'adoption', nor is it just referring to our membership of the family of God. It also incorporates the receiving of an inheritance. Christ is the mediator be-tween God and Man and he stands between the Kingdom and us, mediating between our inheritance and us. Jesus says that there is a great inheritance waiting for you, a Kingdom that is yours, even though you know nothing about it. Jesus says: I am here to reveal it to you and help you to claim it. I am the mediator. I am the Door. Come to me, trust in me, and enter into the place (Kingdom/inheritance) prepared for you. John 14:2 puts it this way: "*My Father's house has many rooms; if that were not so, would I have told you that I am going there to prepare a place for you?*"

When Paul speaks about the 'spirit of adoption', the picture is of a man who has a family business. Naturally, he wants to pass on this business to his son. Typically, such a man would hire a pedagogue (tutor) to take charge of his son's development. For example, if the family business was farming, then the tutor would place the son under the tuition of various skilled artisans in order that the boy would learn the business from top to bottom. The son might spend time, like an apprentice, under the ploughman, the sower, the reapers, the husbandman, the accountant etc. He would learn the skills surrounding buying and selling and, in time, the tutor would declare to the father that his son was ready to take responsibility for the family business. The qualification for the readiness for inheritance was the son's ability to think, speak and act like his father. Once the son had matured in this way, his father would take him to the city gates and declare in front of everybody, "This is my son in whom I'm well pleased. Listen to him". In other words, the man was communicating to the people that when they heard the son speaking, it was as though the father himself was speaking. The son had all authority to sell and all resources to buy. In effect, he was ready to run the family business and his father was publicly 'adopting' him. Throughout the process, the boy was merely an apprentice, but at all times he was the heir to the estate! Paul tells the church in Rome, *"Now if we are children, then we are heirs—heirs of God and co-heirs with Christ, if indeed we share in his sufferings in order that we may also share in his glory."* (Romans 8:17).

This is what making disciples is all about - the Holy Spirit is the pedagogue/tutor and the skilled artisans are the gifts of apostles, prophets, evangelists, pastors and teachers. These gifts are given to the church by Christ *"to equip the saints for works of service, so that the body of Christ may be built up until we all reach unity in the faith and in the knowledge of the Son of God and become mature, attaining to the whole measure of the fullness of Christ."* (Eph. 4:12-13).

Of course the first step is to be born from above (John 3:3). Through Jesus we can enter the door of the Kingdom and begin to live and think and act like who we really are – children of the King. Being born from above is the indispensable step because we cannot see the Kingdom of God, let alone enter it, without becoming a new creation. This involves repentance, believing in Christ, being baptised and receiving the Holy Spirit. However, it is only the first step, albeit an important one. Once through the door of the Kingdom, Jesus says we can have life 'to the full'. We read in John 10:7-10; *"Therefore Jesus said again, "Very truly I tell you, I am the gate for the sheep. All who have come before me are thieves and robbers, but the sheep have not listened to them. I am the gate; whoever enters through me will be saved. They will come in and go out, and find pasture. The thief comes only to steal and kill and destroy; I have come that they may have life, and have it to the full."*

Through the new birth we become citizens of a new country. But is that our experience? If it isn't, then why not? What gospel are we preaching? If the Kingdom of God is so full of promise, power and abundance, then why aren't more people around the world rushing to get in? The answer, I believe, is threefold:

1. People have not heard the message of the Kingdom.
2. Peoples' minds have been blinded so they cannot see the Kingdom.
3. People have heard the wrong message of the Kingdom. In short, the Church is preaching the wrong message!!

Strictly speaking, the word 'Gospel' is not the message itself but rather a description of the message - good news! Jesus never told us to go and simply preach a 'gospel'. There are many kinds of good news we could talk about, but there is only one that Jesus identified as the focus of our preaching. He told us to preach the Gospel of the Kingdom. This good news is not limited to forgiveness and salvation but, of course, it includes that.

Jesus proclaimed the good news that the Kingdom of God had come to earth once again. In other words, we can be part of the age to come. That was

His gospel. It is not a gospel about Jesus, but the gospel according to Jesus. It was not good news about a new religion or denomination. We weren't called to make people feel good with a message that created a warm, safe feeling. Jesus' message was the good news that God's Kingdom had come on Earth and that any who would come would be reunited in spirit and fellowship with him and be restored to their full position and rights as children of God and citizens of His Kingdom. The good news of the kingdom is that we can regain what Adam and Eve lost in the Garden and we can once again assume the place of dominion authority that God intended for us in the beginning. All this can be ours…if we repent! In order to accomplish this, Jesus called us to make disciples, not merely get decisions.

Jesus told us to preach the good news of the Kingdom, yet we have almost exclusively focused our preaching on Jesus as the door. This is the main reason why the church is not more effective. Everyone wants power, but have sought it through money or position. Even people in the church have discovered the King, but have no clue about the Kingdom that he came to bring to mankind. A typical example of what Jesus preached is found in John 3:1-7. In effect, Nicodemus was not asking how he could get to Heaven, but how he could get into the Kingdom and be part of the 'age to come'. That's what he meant by eternal life. In effect, Nicodemus was saying, "I see the Kingdom of God at work in you. How can I get it?" Jesus responded by telling Nicodemus how to enter. However, there is no biblical evidence that Jesus made the "born again" message the focus of His message to the crowds. His message was quite different when dealing with the Scribes and Pharisees who challenged Him. But with the common people, Jesus preached the Kingdom.

Jesus preached the Kingdom in word and demonstrated it in power. Similarly, when we tell people of a domain where there is life, hope, peace, joy, and the power to rise above daily problems and difficulties, and live successfully and victoriously right now, they will say, "Hey, I can relate to that!" It's not just pie in the sky when we die! This is the great challenge to us in our times. The message we preach must be the message that we live. The Kingdom of God has come to Earth. Let all who will, repent and enter in. That's the gospel that Jesus preached and commissioned his followers to preach. However, very often we preach about prosperity, faith, healing, gifts, ministries, and other secondary issues without a Kingdom context. Kingdom is rarely preached.

If I was a chef and you hired me to prepare a turkey with all the trimmings for your guests, but when they sat down you discovered I'd cooked fish and chips instead, what would you think? Was I right or wrong? It was food, wasn't it? We have a tendency to believe that as long as something is not wrong, it must be right! Our problem is that we spend so much time telling people how to get into the Kingdom that we rarely teach them what to do once they get inside. We have to learn to disciple people to conversion and beyond, not just see conversion as a successful conclusion, or consider discipling as a post-conversion only process, but we will discuss this more later.

Because we tend to preach a gospel of salvation alone, people get stuck at the door. Luke 12:32 says that our Father *"is pleased to give you the Kingdom"*. It is what he wants to do. It is what he intended from the beginning. If we get 'stuck' at the door, we will never experience the fullness of the Kingdom that the Father has prepared for us. The Kingdom is a realm where we can experience life to the full! As we have already noted, in John 10:7 Jesus said, *"I am the gate for the sheep"*, but in 10:11 He also said he was *"the Good Shepherd"*. Shepherds do not give their sheep grass; they lead the sheep to where they can find good pasture. Jesus is the shepherd who brings us into the abundant pastures of his Father's Kingdom, but how much nourishment and refreshing we receive there is up to us. The good news that John and Jesus and the early church preached was the good news of the Kingdom. So much of the time today we get the message wrong by preaching the good news of Heaven. The question is, are we escaping the world or changing the world? Actually, God's purpose is to bring Heaven and Earth together in the new Heavens and new Earth. *"But in keeping with his promise we are looking forward to a new heaven and a new earth, where righteousness dwells"* (1 Peter 3:13).

The comfort of heaven helps to keep us and sustain us through the dark hours but it is not, and should never be, the focus of the gospel we preach. Scripture promises us that through Jesus we would overcome the World (1 Jn. 5:4-5), not that he would rescue us from a world on the brink of overcoming us. God is bent on putting this World to rights. Actually, Jesus preached the opposite of much that is preached. He taught that Heaven was coming to Earth. Indeed, that it was already here, and He was its herald. That is why he taught his disciples to pray, *"Your Kingdom come, your will be done on Earth as it is in Heaven"* (Matt 6:9-10). Heaven, however, is not far away. It is the adjacent realm to our own. Any believer who dies is instantaneously there. That's how close God is. When we pray for God's will to be done on Earth, we are asking him to carry out his purpose, to fulfil His original intent. God's original and eternal purpose was to extend his heavenly rule to Earth through human beings.

Chapter 4: A Kingdom of Servant Kings

The Kingdom of God is the only kingdom in which every citizen is related to the King! Their rulership is not over people, but in a specific area of gifting. This is why Jesus is referred to as the King of Kings and Lord of Lords! We are kings who serve the world with our God-given gift. We serve our way into leadership. This is what Jesus meant when He said, *"The greatest among you shall be your servant"* (Matt 23:11). As I have already stated, Jesus' mission consisted of 5 specific goals:

1. He came to reintroduce the Kingdom of Heaven on Earth to Man
2. He came to restore the holiness and righteousness of mankind. *"For the Son of Man came to seek and save the lost"* (Luke 19:10).
3. He came to restore the Holy Spirit in Man.
4. Jesus came to retrain mankind for Kingdom leadership.
5. He came to restore the Kingdom rulership of God on Earth through mankind – to return the administration of God's Kingdom on Earth to God's earthly agents.

At one time, Adam and Eve were the Kingdom of God on Earth, ruling from the Garden of Eden. Heaven and Earth coexisted in the Garden. God's plan had been to rule the Earth through a family called mankind. Adam and Eve's connection to God was the Holy Spirit, who dwelled in them, but their sin corrupted them and made them unholy vessels no longer fit to carry the Holy Spirit. The Spirit departed, taking with him man's only direct connection to God and, therefore, the Earth's only direct connection to the Kingdom of God.

Jesus came to reintroduce the Kingdom and, just as God made woman to be a helper and equal partner to man, so He gave the Holy Spirit to help Man (both male & female) administer His earthly domain in accordance with His will. Whatever God wanted, the Holy Spirit revealed to Man and Man then manifested that will on earth. God wanted His Kingdom rulership to come to Earth, but He could only do this through His children who are connected to Him by the Spirit of God (see 1Corinthians 2:10-13). After the Fall, Man was still on Earth, he was still a spirit inhabiting a flesh and blood body, and he was still designed to dominate the Earth, but the Earth was now dominating him. Man became subject to the very things that he was supposed to rule over. In Jesus Christ, the Holy Spirit returned to Earth to dwell in full force in a human being for the first time since leaving Adam and Eve in the Garden of Eden. The title 'Christ' means the 'Anointed One' – 'For in Christ all the fullness of the Deity lives in bodily form' (Colossians 2:9). That fullness was the Holy Spirit, who was now abiding and dwelling in human flesh again. And so, in essence, we can say that:

Jesus came to reintroduce the Kingdom of Heaven on Earth: It is here now and we need to adjust our thinking, through repentance, to that new reality.

Jesus Came to Restore Holiness and Righteousness to Mankind: A righteous person is some-one who is in right standing with the authorities. Acting right doesn't make one righteous. Righteous-ness is actually a legal term that means to be 'rightly positioned'. When Adam and Eve fell, they fell out of right standing with the sole ruling authority of the Kingdom of Heaven.

Now the blood of Jesus has cleansed our sin and created a basis for our forgiveness, making it possible for Christ to restore us to righteousness and holiness and bring us the Holy Spirit. This is why religion that denies Jesus has a problem. Without Jesus, we do not have His blood to cleanse our sin, and without the cleansing of our sin we cannot become holy. Unless we become holy, we cannot receive the Holy Spirit, and unless we receive the Holy Spirit, we cannot become citizens of the Kingdom of God. Only blood can cover sin. Adam and Eve tried to cover themselves with leaves, but that was inadequate because no blood was involved. That's why God covered them with animal skins, although animal sacrifice was only a symbol of covered sin – a foreshadowing of the ultimate, total and complete sacrifice of the Lamb of God. So, the Kingdom is not a religion be-cause religion is man's search for God. With the Kingdom the search is over. Of all the faith systems in the world, the

Kingdom of God alone is effective because it alone has the blood of Christ, which takes away the sin of man. It alone has the spirit of God dwelling in the lives of believers. It alone can restore us to righteousness and holiness.

Jesus came to restore the Holy Spirit in Man: Why is the Holy Spirit so important? As we have seen before, He is the link, the spiritual connection between us and the Kingdom of God. Jesus is the baptiser in the Holy Spirit and he released the Holy Spirit to His disciples as a continuing indwelling presence. By this act, Jesus returned to mankind that which Adam and Eve had lost in the Gar-den. The link was restored. However, we must be retrained in the behaviour and mindset of the Kingdom. In this task, the Holy Spirit is our tutor, like the pedagogue that the father in our earlier ex-ample engaged to prepare his child for his inheritance. In his earthly incarnation, Jesus could not be continuously and physically present with all His followers, so He promised to send His Spirit who would abide with us forever and teach us how to think, act and speak like the Father - like the royalty we are (John 14:16-17, 26 and 16:7, 13).

Typically, the sons and daughters of a king or queen are brought up in a special way that prepares them for their roles as royalty. For example in the UK, Princes William and Harry are being carefully prepared for life as potential future kings. Prince William is learning everything he needs so that if and when the day comes, he will be able to sit on the throne as the king. As royal children of our heavenly Father, we can take charge of our circumstances, rather than being a slave to them. We can live daily in power and victory, rather than in weakness and defeat. All it takes is training - and the Holy Spirit is our teacher.

Jesus sent the Holy Spirit to continue his work of retraining mankind for Kingdom leader-ship: In every word, action, and moment of His life on Earth, Jesus showed us what the Father is like and thus what we should be like as His children. If we want to know what we should be like as children of the Father, all we have to do is look at Jesus who is the only begotten Son of the Father. The Holy Spirit in us enables us to understand what we see in Jesus and what we hear in His teachings, and gives us the power to carry them over into our lives. We have been slaves for so long that we don't know how to handle freedom – a bit like the elephant chained to a post or the tiger held in a cage for a long time continues their restrictive behaviour even after being released. In Rom. 12:1-2 Paul says that we should not allow ourselves any longer to be moulded by the World we have lived in all our lives, but to be transformed by the renewing of our minds to think and conform to the mind of Christ.

So, we can say that Jesus came to restore the Kingdom of Heaven and kingdom rulership on earth: He demonstrated the truth that God's Kingdom had come to Earth and each of us who are 'in Christ' are called and are being equipped as kings and priests to represent that Kingdom before the rest of the World. God intends us to be His representative rulers - His ambassadors or vice-regents; over the rest of the created order. We are to be priest-kings on the Earth. As priests, we represent God's nature and character, and as kings we display His Kingdom government. We may call it 'training for reigning', more commonly referred to as 'discipleship'.

The future of our planet depends on us responding to Jesus' command to make disciples. In Romans chapter 8, we see 3 'groanings': we groan as we await our new resurrection bodies; the Holy Spirit groans as He helps us in our weakness through prayer; and, in verse 22, the whole creation has been groaning in labour pains. It waits with eager longing for the revelation of the children of God (v 19). Somehow, the restoration of planet Earth is linked to a restored mankind. The creation was once managed by Adam and Eve but, since the Fall, it has been desperately mismanaged by man - hence the mess we find ourselves in! But God does not scrap what he declares to be good. Rather, he is going to restore it to its original pristine condition and that is why verse 20 says that God 'subjected it in hope' - the hope of restoration. Therefore, we must think in terms of all of creation being saved, or restored, not just man.

The Roman church was a mixture of Jews and Gentiles and, as a result, it was riddled with division. Paul writes to the believers there and, in Romans 8, he says that salvation is not just for the Jew and the Gentile, but for the whole creation. Now since all of creation eagerly awaits the revealing of the children of God, the implication is that they (we) are somehow instrumental in its restoration.

Chapter 5: Kings, Prophets and the Kingdom

In reading Exodus 19:6, Psalms 22:28, 45:6, 145:11, and Daniel 2:44, we can see that God's plan is to reverse and destroy the works of the Devil and fully restore His rule over the earthly realm through His human representatives. In other words, he is going to restore all that was lost in the Garden of Eden as declared through His prophets. Everyone, it seems, understood the priority of the Kingdom; everyone, that is, except us! In recent years, the focus in much of the Body of Christ has shifted away from the Kingdom of God to other issues. The tragic result is that multitudes of believers today know little about the Kingdom, and even fewer understand their place and rights and responsibilities as Kingdom citizens.

Kingdom assumes a king and King David understood that human kingdoms are temporary, but God's Kingdom is eternal (see Psalm 10:16). David, Israel's second and greatest king, praised and acknowledged the Lord as the 'King of Glory'. The word 'glory' literally means 'heavy' or 'weighty', especially when referring to someone of great importance or high esteem. With the phrase 'King of Glory', David exalts God as the greatest King of all and worthy of the highest esteem. Many earthly kings have ruled over their subjects with cruelty and oppression, but Psalm 45:6 says that the thing that defines the rule of King Jesus is 'justice'. Now, David understood his role not only as a king un-der God with civic responsibilities to his people, but also as a priest before God with spiritual responsibilities on behalf of his people. Like David, we are called to rule as kings in this world as well as to fulfil the priestly role of carrying out our spiritual care of the people in the earthly regions. (A priest may be defined as 'one who stands between God and man to minister').

The psalmists weren't the only people to understand the kingship of God. Isaiah 6:1-5 is a powerful depiction of a king on his throne. The prophet also experienced the merciful justice of God in Isaiah 6:6-8:

6 *Then one of the seraphim flew to me with a live coal in his hand, which he had taken with tongs from the altar.*
7 *With it he touched my mouth and said, "See, this has touched your lips; your guilt is taken away and your sin atoned for."*
8 *Then I heard the voice of the Lord saying, "Whom shall I send? And who will go for us?"*
And I said, "Here am I. Send me!"

Once he had experienced the cleansing of his sin, the power of his vision inspired him to respond to the King's call. Isaiah became an ambassador for the Lord Almighty, called and appointed to proclaim the message of the Kingdom of God. What is this Kingdom like? It is a realm ruled by a God who is mighty and everlasting, and who is a Wonderful Counsellor (a wise and just Judge); a realm characterised by peace, justice and righteousness (Isaiah 9:6-7).

Chapter 7 of the book of Daniel is extremely important to understanding both the Kingdom and the End Times. The four beasts, and the fourth one in particular I believe, represent the forces of darkness that lie behind the power, wickedness and corruption of many kingdoms of the World. However, in verse 13, we see *"one like a son of man, coming with the clouds of heaven"*. In verse14 it goes on to say that *"His dominion is an everlasting dominion that will not pass away, and His Kingdom is one that will never be destroyed"*.

"But the holy people of the Most High will receive the Kingdom and will possess it forever - yes, for ever and ever." (Daniel 7:8). Through his death on the cross and resurrection from the dead, Jesus the Son of Man conquered Satan and broke his power and authority forever. The result of this victory is announced in verse 14: *"He was given authority, glory and sovereign power; all nations and peoples of every language worshiped him."* This picture is very similar to Paul's words in Philippians 2:8-11 where *"Every knee will bow and every tongue confess that Jesus Christ is Lord."*

This whole scenario, clearly stated in Daniel 7:18, is further underlined in verses. 22 to 27:

"...until the Ancient of Days came and pronounced judgment in favour of the holy people of the Most High, and the time came when they possessed the Kingdom...Then the sovereignty, power and greatness of all the kingdoms under Heaven will be handed over to the holy people of the Most High. His kingdom will be an everlasting kingdom, and all rulers will worship and obey him."

What we lost at the Fall was not Heaven, but the Kingdom. Jesus died on the cross and rose from the dead not so much to take us to Heaven as to bring us back into possession of the Kingdom on Earth that we lost. When we receive it, we will possess it forever and ever. Verse 27 mentions three specific things we receive:

Sovereignty – within the scope of our delegated sovereignty, we have absolute authority.

Dominion - when we are restored to the Kingdom, we are restored to greatness. Jesus said that the key to true greatness is humility and service. We were not created to dominate each other or to be dominated, but to serve one another equally as kings and priests in our Father's Kingdom.

Power – power to overcome, prosper, live in victory, be joyful, and fulfil our potential.

Chapter 6: The Priority of the Kingdom

Someone once said, "The greatest discovery is self-discovery". In truth, the spiritual world is more real than the natural one. First of all, the spiritual realm is larger than the physical realm and, secondly, it is the realm from which the physical realm originated. In other words, the invisible produced the visible. Psalm 115:16 says that God gave us this planet, *"The highest heavens belong to the Lord, but the Earth He has given to man".* Ever since Adam's fall, God has been executing His plan to restore mankind to his place of dominion. Immediately after the Fall God said to Satan, *"I will put enmity between you and the woman, and between your offspring and hers; He will crush your head, and you will strike His heel"* (Gen. 3:15). Here the word 'head' refers to authority.

The terms 'Son of Man' and 'Ancient of Days' are found in Daniel 7:13-14 where it speaks of one like the Son of Man, coming with the clouds of Heaven. This is a reference, not to literal clouds in the sky, but to hosts of angels and great glory. The Jews regarded this son of man as a reference to the Messiah, the Anointed One whom God would send to deliver His people. This is why the religious leaders of his day were so angry with Jesus. The thought that Messiah would violate the Sabbath law by healing people (working) was blasphemous. And yet in John 5:16-19 Jesus says that his Father is always at work and he was just copying Him.

The important point here is that Jesus, as the Son of His Father, was committed to working when-ever His Father worked, and doing whatever His Father was doing. Besides this, Jesus plainly said, *"The Sabbath was made for Man, not Man for the Sabbath. So the Son of Man is Lord even of the Sabbath"* (Mark 2:7-28).

When we claim someone as father, we claim him as the source of who we are, suggesting we are made of the same 'stuff'. This is what Jesus was claiming, which is why He was persecuted. See what Jesus said in John 5:21-27:

"For just as the Father raises the dead and gives them life, even so the Son gives life to whom he is pleased to give it. Moreover, the Father judges no one, but has entrusted all judgment to the Son, that all may honour the Son just as they honour the Father. Whoever does not honour the Son does not honour the Father, who sent him. Very truly I tell you, whoever hears my word and believes him who sent me has eternal life and will not be judged but has crossed over from death to life. Very truly I tell you, a time is coming and has now come when the dead will hear the voice of the Son of God and those who hear will live. For as the Father has life in himself, so he has granted the Son also to have life in himself. And he has given him authority to judge because he is the Son of Man."

It is significant that Jesus refers to himself as the 'Son of God' in relation to His authority to give life and as the 'Son of Man' in relation to His authority to judge. No one except Jesus has ever met this qualification, but he met it perfectly. Born of a woman, born of a virgin, born into the ancestral line of David, Jesus was 'Son of Man' because he was fully human. He was, as Paul says in 1 Corinthians 15:45, the last 'Adam'. Unlike the first Adam, Jesus perfectly fulfilled God's original plan and accomplished what Adam could not. Because he fulfilled his Father's will perfectly and was without sin, Jesus, the Son of Man, was qualified to judge the human race. He passed that judgement at the cross where he bore our sin guilt, becoming sin for us (see 2 Corinthians 5:21), and sentenced Himself to death. After judging our sin as the Son of Man, he was able, as the Son of God, to give us life. Everything Jesus did in his earthly ministry - healing the sick, raising the dead, casting out demons, calming storms, feeding multitudes - he did under his authority as the Son of Man, empowered by the Holy Spirit. In a similar way, God gave dominion over the Earth to mankind. That is why whenever God wants to do something in the physical realm of Earth, He seeks to work through human agents. In Jesus, He has the perfect man to initiate His work. In Christ, we are authorised to rule on earth because we are human, just as he was.

However, our greatest enemy is ignorance. We don't know what we don't know, and what we don't know is killing us; or at least depriving us of a full and abundant life. The antidote for ignorance is knowledge, and so God sent us His Word. It is a matter of grooming our Kingdom mentality, of learning to think and talk like our Father, and learning to act like the royalty we are rather than like the galley slaves the devil has told us we are. Unfortunately, this is not a natural mindset for us, and most believers have trouble making the adjustment. However, God is building a kingdom of priests and kings on Earth; not two separate classes or castes, but two offices combined in the same person. Except for Jesus Christ, such a combination had not existed since Adam, but it has always been God's plan.

"Now if you obey me fully and keep my covenant, then out of all nations you will be my treasured possession. Although the whole earth is mine, you will be for me a kingdom of priests and a holy nation.' These are the words you are to speak to the Israelites." (Exodus 19:5-6)

'A royal priesthood' (1 Peter 2:9-10) is another way of saying that each one of us is both a king and a priest. We are God's agents, called to lead those still trapped in darkness into the wonderful light of His Kingdom. Paul described this special calling this way:

"Therefore, if anyone is in Christ, the new creation has come; the old has gone, the new is here! All this is from God, who reconciled us to himself through Christ and gave us the ministry of reconciliation: That God was reconciling the World to himself in Christ, not counting people's sins against them. And he has committed to us the message of reconciliation. We are therefore Christ's ambassadors, as though God were making his appeal through us. We implore you on Christ's behalf: Be reconciled to God. God made him who had no sin to be sin for us, so that in him we might be-come the righteousness of God." (2 Cor. 5:17-21).

Jesus command to us today is the same as that which he gave to His disciples 2000 years ago: *"As you go, preach this message: The kingdom of heaven is near (has arrived)"* (Matt 10:7).

Now we can go on to examine in more detail God's Eternal Purpose.

Chapter 7: The Eternal Purpose

"In the beginning God created the heavens and the Earth" (Gen. 1:1 NIV).

Genesis 1 and 2 deal with beginnings. They set forth an introduction to God, the beginning of creation, the beginning of humanity, and an outline of the eternal purpose of God.

Actually, these first two chapters of Genesis and the last two chapters of Revelation are the only ones in the whole Bible where there is no sin, no fall and no curse. They mirror one another, and the entire Bible is the unfolding drama of all the themes of Genesis 1 and 2. One can follow them through until their consummation in Revelation 21 and 22. There is a golden thread running through from Genesis to Revelation that can be summed up in three words: 'The Eternal Purpose'.

Nearly everyone looks upon the book of Revelation as a book of insoluble mystery. It deals with the end of this age as people normally understand it. The book of Genesis is just as wonderful and mysterious, for it deals with the beginning of human existence and provides us with a key that helps us understand many of the mysteries of life.

In Ephesians 3:11, the apostle Paul writes, *"This was according to The Eternal Purpose which He accomplished in Christ Jesus our Lord"*. This eternal purpose is the governing theme of the whole Bible and it is the reason why God created in the first place. In his book 'From Eternity to Here' author Frank Viola identifies four concepts that he believes constitute this eternal purpose, and they are found in the following passages:

- In Ephesians 2:13-22, Paul refers to the church as a body (verse 16), a family or household (verse 19), and a dwelling or house (verse 22).

- In Ephesians 5: 25-32, the apostle refers to the Church as a bride/ wife.

- In Ephesians 3:10-11 we read…"*His intent was that now, through the church, the manifold wisdom of God should be made known to the rulers and authorities in the heavenly realms, according to his eternal purpose that he accomplished in Christ Jesus our Lord.*"

Now, in his book, Viola refers to the series of six 'Star Wars' movies (and, at the time of writing this, the seventh has just been released). Frank Viola observes that the first episode was released in 1977, the second in 1980, and the third in 1983. Later, after a long period, three prequels were made. So, we could say that the final three movies were actually the first ones even though they weren't made until 1999, 2002 and 2005. The point that Viola makes is that one didn't really understand what was going on in the first movies in full context until you saw episodes 1 to 3 later. It's the same way we are trained to understand God's eternal purpose. Most Christians today think that God's purpose is to 'save the lost' and 'make the world a better place'.

There is much more, but the reason we think this way is because we start the story in the wrong place i.e. in Genesis 3 - the Fall of Man (a bit like starting with Episode 4 of Star Wars). Therefore, we conclude that we've got to redeem people and restore the world - hence the Gospel of Salvation.

Before we examine the eternal purpose in a little more detail, I want to look at three points that Frank Viola makes regarding Genesis 1 and 2:

1. God is introduced – no attempt is made to prove the existence of God. God is introduced as one who has existed from all eternity. He is behind all things, before all things, and above all things. He is the eternal and changeless God
2. The Earth is explained - Genesis declares that the earth and our universe were created by God. Matter is not eternal. It was not perfect at the beginning, but as the Spirit of God moved upon it, God was able to say that "it is good." We must never forget that God created everything "good".
3. Man is interpreted - In Psalms 8 verse 4, the psalmist raised the question: "What is man?" The first two chapters of Genesis leave no doubt that Man is a special creation. He is the crown and climax of God's creative activity, made in the image of God. We are not to understand this as referring to a physical likeness to God but rather to the capabilities of knowing, responding to, and having immediate fellowship with God. In their rational, moral, and spiritual nature, people can

walk and talk with God and come to resemble him in a manner impossible to other earthly creatures. God planned for Man's life to be one of joyful activity. God gave him beautiful surroundings, beloved companionship, and a pleasant occupation. Combined with these was the joy of communion with God. This is where the gospel starts, not the Fall of chapter 3.

Now, back to the eternal purpose of Ephesians 3:11: We have seen that God created a good, not-fallen, world. The story begins in Genesis 1 and 2, not chapter 3. It's not that saving people and making the world a better place is not important, it is. It's just not God's highest intention, not His eternal purpose. Now, back to the four words we highlighted earlier:

A Family
A Body
A House
A Bride

We should note that these things are primarily for God, not for us. God wanted something and this was His provocation for creation.

First of all, God wants a family: He wants many children to populate and rule (look after) the Earth. As we have already seen, God wants a family of kings and priests to act as vice-regents of his kingdom on Earth. He starts by creating the first man and woman and then commands them to be fruitful, multiply and fill the earth (Genesis 1:28). This is the threefold purpose and destiny of man:

fruitfulness, multiplication and authority/ dominion which we will explore in more detail later.

Now, Jesus is God's ONLY begotten Son, but Adam was also called 'the son of God' and the Bible tells us that man was made in the image and likeness of God. The nation of Israel was also referred to as God's son and called to be God's family as well as His Bride. Abraham, the father of Israel, was told by God, *"all peoples on Earth will be blessed through you"* (Genesis 12:3). Unfortunately, Israel failed in their calling because they took the blessings and kept them to themselves, thinking that they were the object rather than the means of God's purposes.

Then Jesus appeared on earth. He is the first one to call God his father, which of course was regarded as blasphemy by the religious leaders of the day. Jesus is the ONLY begotten son but, as we have already noted, God's eternal purpose was to have a family. The Bible says that *"unless a kernel of wheat falls to the ground and dies, it remains only a single seed. But if it dies, it produces many seeds"* (John 12:24). And so, Jesus is put to death, but three days later He rises from the grave and Paul says, *"So it is written: "The first man Adam became a living being"; the last Adam, a life-giving spirit"* (1 Corinthians 15:45). He breathes the Holy Spirit into his disciples and he be-comes the *"firstborn among many brothers"* (Romans 8:29). Interestingly, Jesus referred to his disciples as brothers on resurrection morning when he told Mary Magdalene: *"Do not hold on to me, for I have not yet ascended to the Father. Go instead to my brothers and tell them, 'I am ascending to my Father and your Father, to my God and your God."* (John 20:17). And so, now God has a family.

<u>Secondly, God required a body</u> through which to express himself. Going back to the creation story we see that God created Adam and Eve in His image. This then made him 'visible'. Later, he selected a people and his intention was that they be a kingdom of priests. As we have already noted, Israel failed in their calling.

Then Jesus came to complete Israel's story: Hebrews 10:5 says: "Therefore, when Christ came into the world, he said: *"Sacrifice and offering you did not desire, but a <u>body</u> you prepared for me;"* Jesus redefined Israel as himself and succeeded where the nation failed. He is the true Israel, the perfect Priest and King. Since Jesus is *"the image of the invisible God, the Firstborn over all creation"* (Colossians 1:15), he has dominion over the Earth. When Jesus died, it was not only for sin but also to increase his body (John 12:24). So, we are now his body and our purpose is to bear the image of the One who indwells it. If you want to see what God looks like, look at Jesus. However, he is not visible right now, so instead look at his body when it is functioning properly in a given place; every member fruitful, faithful, functioning, multiplying, walking in authority and making Jesus famous!

<u>Thirdly, God wants a house for himself</u>: I know this sound strange, but Frank Viola explains it this way:

Just like Noah, Abraham, Isaac and Jacob were all men of the altar and the tent, so God wants a dwelling place. He instructed Moses to make a tent for Him (the tabernacle). But surely God isn't homeless? After all, he says, *"Heaven is my throne and the Earth is my footstool. Where is the house you will build for me? Where will my resting place be?"* (Isaiah 66:1). Actually, God is building himself a house made out of 'living stones', and this is the provocation for creation.

In Genesis we see that there are building materials in the Garden of Eden and God is living there together with Adam and Eve (the Tree of Life is there). The Garden should be the pattern for the earth - Heaven and Earth together - a house for God. Let us look at some of the many instances that allude to this in the Bible:

- In Genesis 28:12 Jacob sees a stairway and in verses 16-17 he says, *"Surely the Lord is in this place, and I was not aware of it."* He was afraid and said, *"How awesome is this place! This is none other than the house of God; this is the gate of heaven."* Here we see Heaven and Earth coming together as a stairway connects the floors in a home. It is like God is saying, *"I want my house back"!*
- Moses was instructed to build the tabernacle in the wilderness where God's presence would be.
- Solomon built a temple made of gold and precious stones where God presenced himself.

- As the story continues, the house is getting bigger - until the return from the Babylonian exile! However, even then the prophet sees a massive temple and declares that *"The glory of this latter temple shall be greater than the former,' says the Lord of Hosts."* (Haggai 2:9).
- Then Jesus arrives and redefines the house of God (the Temple) as himself. In fact, he tells Nathaniel, *"Most assuredly, I say to you, hereafter you shall see heaven open, and the angels of God ascending and descending upon the Son of Man."* (John 1:51). In essence he was saying that he was the reality, the real stairway to heaven, the real house of God. Elsewhere Jesus said, *"Destroy this temple, and in three days I will raise it up."* (John 2:19).
- Then Jesus is crucified, but three days later the Temple is raised. Another 50 days later, at Pentecost, the Spirit is poured out and the House gets a lot bigger (120 in the upper room and 3000 later the same day). The tongues of fire represent the presence of God in his house and from then on, it's exponential multiplication all the way!

The apostle Peter says *"you also, as living stones, are being built up a spiritual house, a holy priesthood, to offer up spiritual sacrifices acceptable to God through Jesus Christ."* (1 Peter 2:5). God's purpose is not for individual 'living stones', but stones which *"also are being built together for a dwelling place of God in the Spirit."* (Ephesians 2:22). The Lord doesn't just want visitation rights, he wants to live (dwell) in his house. He is the total owner of the house, not a timeshare owner. The house of God - where Heaven and Earth meet!!

Fourthly, the Father wants a Bride for His Son: The Lord God said, *"It is not good for the man to be alone. I will make a helper suitable for him."* (Gen. 2:18). In verse 21, God took Eve out of Adam's side. There was a woman inside the man all the time, and then the two become one again. Verse 24 is a picture of marriage. In fact, throughout the Scriptures we see the principle of marriage, bridegroom and bride, culminating in the marriage of the Lamb:

- Abraham and Sarah - God restores Sarah's youth so that she is able to bear a son even in her old age. This speaks of the restoration of a bride.
- Isaac and Rebekah - the servant, sent to find a bride for Abraham's son, speaks only of Isaac (the child of promise, the only begotten, the one who is to be sacrificed). Even though she had not seen him, Rebekah fell in love with Isaac through the testimony of the servant.
- Jacob and Rachel - Jacob falls in love with a girl at a well. He has 12 sons who become 12 tribes and his name is changed to Israel. Israel ends up in Egypt and after 400 years God causes an Exodus. Beulah land becomes Israel's wife/ bride - they are married to the land.
- Time and time again brides keep appearing: In Song of Songs, Psalms, in Proverbs and, finally, in the New Testament; reality appears. In the gospels, John the Baptist introduces the Bridegroom, the Son of Man (Hebrew Adam). Jesus is the new or last Adam. He is the new Israel: he comes out of Egypt (Hosea); his 40

days of temptation parallel Israel's 40 years in the wilder-ness; the 12 disciples parallel the 12 tribes of Israel. In John 4, by Jacob's well, Jesus breaks every custom of the day. He, a man, speaks to a woman. She is not just any woman, but a Samaritan (half Jew, half Gentile in the same body!!) She has been divorced five times and is living with number six.

Jesus is therefore the seventh Man in her life. He shares all sorts of wonderful things with her, and then He eats the Samaritan food and accepts their hospitality (Jn. 4:40). This is completely against Jewish custom. A Jewish man, especially a Rabbi, would not converse with a woman in public, or transgress Jewish food laws. Who is this woman? She is you and me: Jew and Gentile in one body, part of the eternal purpose of God. Speaking of Jew and Gentile, Paul writes, *"For he himself is our peace, who has made the two groups one and has destroyed the barrier, the dividing wall of hostility"* (Ephesians 2:14). This is a wonderful picture of the body and the Bride of Christ.

- Then the last Adam goes up a hill and, like the first Adam, God puts Him in the deepest sleep of all – death! As the spear goes in, out of His side comes forth a Bride (the real Eve). We were in Christ since before the foundation of the World in the same way that Eve was in Adam. All the other brides in the Old Testament were just the foreshadowing, the cameo, and an example of the real Bride.

Of course, typically, a bride is only a bride for a certain period of time after which she takes on the role of a wife. Even a cursory glance at the wife described in Proverbs 31 will give us a deeper understanding of our role now and in the age to come. She is depicted as:

- Trustworthy and Productive (v 11)
- A Willing Worker (v 13)
- Inventive (v 14)
- A Provider (v 15)
- Entrepreneurial (v 16)
- Compassionate (v 20)
- Creative (v 22)
- Bringing Glory to her Husband (v 23)
- Wise (v 26)
- God-Fearing (v 30)
- Having an Incredible Reputation (v 31)

In conclusion, the New Jerusalem of Revelation 21 and 22 is where there is neither Jew nor Gentile, rich nor poor, slave nor freeman, male nor female. Revelation 21:2 says *"Then I, John, saw the holy city, the New Jerusalem, coming down out of Heaven from God, prepared as a bride adorned for her husband"*.

1st Century Christians understood that they were not of this world although they were made for it. They were a colony of Heaven on Earth. They were a new city - a city of God. They were counter-cultural, living as real community and family. They took care of each other and there was peace in that community and justice in the family. It was a microcosm of the Kingdom of God in the midst of a fallen, broken world and people could look and see that it was the Kingdom of Heaven on this earth. Heaven and Earth met in these people and they were not using political power, the power of Caesar, but the Power of God. The world had never seen Jews and Gentiles living together, and now here they were arm-in-arm, singing together. It's because they are following the new Lord of this world! He is the new Emperor and He is the true Israel and the new, true kind of human. This Emperor really is divine and these people were living by His life.

This takes us to the end of the story. In Revelation 21 and 22 we see out of the heavens, a building. Man and God are now dwelling together. However, it's not just a building or house, it's a garden, a garden city. There are trees, and the Tree of Life (Christ) is there, and there is a river (Christ). This city is also a Bride who loves her Bridegroom because He first loved her and gave Himself for her. Finally, this city is not only a Bride, but it is also a family and a body, a living organism.

This is also a picture of the Church. What's more, in every city on this planet, God wants such an example…a miniature of the New Jerusalem. A Body, fully functioning. A Bride, loving and being loved by Jesus. A family and the house of God where Heaven and Earth intersect. In conclusion, a corporate expression of Jesus Christ.

Chapter 7: Fruitfulness, Multiplication and Dominion

Around 15 years ago my wife and I travelled to Bogota, Colombia with a number of leaders from our then church in Preston, Lancashire. The purpose of our trip was to visit the huge and thriving church, 'Mision Charismatica Internacional', led by Pastor Cesar Castellanos. Whilst there, we attended an international conference and participated in the church. Central to their culture was the teaching of fruitfulness, multiplication and authority which we might understand as God's threefold purpose and destiny for His people.

When God speaks something over our lives, we need to sit up and take notice because God's words have the power of creation and life in them. Personal prophecies can be encouraging, but God's words are 'more sure'. In the Bible, we see that God has spoken a threefold purpose and blessing over every man and woman. It is not some kind of wish list, but a creative order whereby God will get what He wants: His Kingdom on Earth through a family, a house, a body and a Bride in his image.

'Then God said, "Let the land produce vegetation: Seed-bearing plants and trees on the land that bear fruit with seed in it, according to their various kinds." And it was so. The land produced vegetation: plants bearing seed according to their kinds and trees bearing fruit with seed in it according to

their kinds. And God saw that it was good." (Genesis 1:11-12).

In these verses we see the creative order established: fruitfulness produces seed, and seed leads to multiplication. Later in the same chapter we see this principle applied to man, with the addition of dominion or authority.

"So God created mankind in his own image, in the image of God he created them; male and female he created them. God blessed them and said to them, "Be fruitful and increase in number; fill the earth and subdue it. Rule over the fish in the sea and the birds in the sky and over every living creature that moves on the ground."" (Genesis 1:27-28).

So, we can see that man was created and inherently endued with this threefold purpose - and what God commands, He equips for. We can describe fruitfulness as character development and holiness or Christlikeness. Multiplication speaks for itself and refers to numerical growth. Finally, authority or dominion refers to our becoming the sons of God or, as we have already seen, receiving the spirit of adoption. This authority can extend to spiritual warfare, teaching others, healing the sick, casting out demons and establishing Kingdom order by leading.

We can see the importance of this command and blessing in that it is mentioned at the creation of mankind. However, its importance is magnified exponentially when we see that there were four very significant times when God spoke this purpose:

- To Adam when He created man.

- To Noah at the re-beginning of mankind.
- To Abraham at the creation of a holy nation.
- To the disciples at the creation of the church.

Firstly, let us look at Adam in more detail. It was the beginning of mankind and, in Genesis 1:28, God commands Adam to be fruitful, multiply and exercise dominion. Actually, this purpose and blessing was even operational in fallen mankind as we see at the tower of Babel in Genesis 11:6:

"The Lord said, "If as one people speaking the same language they have begun to do this, then nothing they plan to do will be impossible for them"."

As a result, God had to place limitations on them - He confused their language. This had the result that they were not able to work in unity (speak the same language). If only we realised the power inherent in us under God and worked together in unity to release it! This is what Jesus prayed for: That we might be one!

Now, secondly, let us look at Genesis 9:2, where God speaks to Noah at the rebirth of mankind:

"Then God blessed Noah and his sons, saying to them, "Be fruitful and increase in number and fill the Earth. The fear and dread of you will fall on all the beasts of the earth, and on all the birds in the sky, on every creature that moves along the ground, and on all the fish in the sea; they are given into your hands."

Here, we see a repeat of what was spoken over Adam. In other words, God has not changed his mind nor the process through which he will get what he wants, namely his kingdom on earth through a family, a house, a body and a Bride in his image.

The third occasion we see this threefold blessing repeated is in Genesis 17:5-7, when God speaks to a man called Abram at the birth of a holy nation, Israel:

"When Abram was ninety-nine years old, the Lord appeared to him and said, "I am God Almighty; walk before me faithfully and be blameless. Then I will make my covenant between me and you and will greatly increase your numbers." Abram fell facedown, and God said to him, No longer will you be called Abram; your name will be Abraham, for I have made you a father of many nations. I will make you very fruitful; I will make nations of you, and kings will come from you. I will establish my covenant as an everlasting covenant between me and you and your descendants after you for the generations to come, to be your God and the God of your descendants after you."

In verse 1, Abram is told to be faithful and blameless (fruitfulness); in verse 2, God says he will greatly increase Abram's numbers (multiplication). In fact, his name is changed from Abram (exalted father) to Abraham (father of many nations) as part of the covenant. Finally, the Lord says in verse 6 that 'kings shall come from you' (authority). Of course, the notable kings that come through Abraham's line are David and Jesus. Here we see a holy line established as the threefold blessing and purpose is passed on to all the patriarchs (and beyond):

- To Isaac (Genesis 26:3-5, 12-16)
- To Jacob (Genesis 28:3-4)
- Worked through to Israel (Exodus 1:7)

Also, through Jesus, all who belong to him are priests and kings, which brings us to the fourth significant occasion in Matthew 28:18-20 which we call the Great Commission and was, in effect, the creation of a new race - the sons of God:

"Then Jesus came to them and said, "All authority in Heaven and on Earth has been given to me. Therefore go and make disciples of all nations, baptising them in the name of the Father and of the Son and of the Holy Spirit, and teaching them to obey everything I have commanded you. And surely I am with you always, to the very end of the age.""

Jesus has all authority in Heaven and Earth. This authority is given to him by the Father. If this is true, then the next words out of his mouth are important for us to hear. In verse 19 Jesus tells the disciples to make disciples of all nations (multiplication) and, in verse 20, he tells them to teach these followers to obey all he has commanded (to become fruitful). In John 20:21 we read, *"Again Jesus said, "Peace be with you! As the Father has sent me, I am sending you.""*

Fruitfulness Examined

Fruitfulness is an extremely important principle in the Bible. It seems as though everything stems from it. Consider the verses below:

John 15:8: *"This is to my Father's glory, that you bear much fruit, showing yourselves to be my disciples."*

John 15:16: *"You did not choose me, but I chose you and appointed you so that you might go and bear fruit—fruit that will last—and so that whatever you ask in my name the Father will give you."*

It appears that fruitfulness is something that the Lord holds in very high regard. As already mentioned, fruitfulness can be described as character, development, and holiness or Christlikeness. Now, this appears to be a tough calling, but Jesus explained that it will happen automatically as long as we abide in Him. Psalm 1:1-3 has something to say on the matter:

"Blessed is the one who does not walk in step with the wicked or stand in the way that sinners take or sit in the company of mockers, but whose delight is in the law of the Lord, and who meditates on his law day and night. That person is like a tree planted by streams of water, which yields its fruit in season and whose leaf does not wither — whatever they do prospers."

There needs to be nourishment, but there will also be times of pruning in order to maximise fruitfulness. Many people equate the term 'you shall not' with legalism, but there are such things that, although not forbidden, are nevertheless a hindrance to fruitfulness. Also, the Bible says that *"we also, since we are surrounded by so great a cloud of witnesses, let us lay aside every weight, and the sin which so easily ensnares us, and let us run with endurance the race that is set before us"* (Hebrews 12:1). The voice of our spirit is known as conscience – effectively, God has put a 'no' in us. Sometimes it is easier to hear God say, "No" than to hear more positive guidance. If we are going to be fruitful there are going to be things that we need to avoid. God will prune in the areas of values, company, attitudes and motivations.

Isaiah 11:1-2 gives us great hope:

"There shall come forth a Rod from the stem of Jesse, and a Branch shall grow out of his roots. The Spirit of the Lord shall rest upon Him, the Spirit of wisdom and understanding, the Spirit of counsel and might, the Spirit of knowledge and of the fear of the Lord."

It seems that God can produce fruitfulness from a stump. All he needs is a root or a stem. We may not feel that we have a lot to offer him, but God can take what we offer and produce a proliferation of fruit. Basically, what we are talking about here is the purity and holiness of Jesus himself. Christlikeness that is produced in the born again spirit by the Holy Spirit. That's the fruitfulness that is mentioned in Galatians 5:22-23:

"But the fruit of the Spirit is love, joy, peace, longsuffering, kindness, goodness, faithfulness, gentleness, self-control. Against such there is no law."

Fruitfulness is, first and foremost, an issue of the heart! Apple trees have no problem producing apples and, in the same way, sinners have no problem producing sin. By the same token, Christ followers should have no problem producing spiritual fruit. Matthew 12:33-35 puts it like this:

"Either make the tree good and its fruit good, or else make the tree bad and its fruit bad; for a tree is known by its fruit. Brood of vipers! How can you, being evil, speak good things? For out of the abundance of the heart the mouth speaks. A good man out of the good treasure of his heart brings forth good things, and an evil man out of the evil treasure brings forth evil things."

Being fruitful is simply a matter of abiding, but it does require a total giving of oneself. Consider the following verses:

"I am the vine, you are the branches. He who abides in Me, and I in him, bears much fruit; for with-out Me you can do nothing." (John 15:5).

"I beseech you therefore, brethren, by the mercies of God, that you present your bodies a living sacrifice, holy, acceptable to God, which is your reasonable service. And do not be conformed to this world, but be transformed by the renewing of your mind, that you may prove what is that good and acceptable and perfect will of God." (Romans 12:1-2).

The gospel… *"which has come to you, as it has also in all the world, and is bringing forth fruit, as it is also among you since the day you heard and knew the grace of God in truth…"* (Colossians 1:6)

We will look further into fruitfulness later as we examine what Mike Breen says through his 'LifeShapes' ideas. Fruitfulness through abiding in Christ is really dependent on establishing healthy rhythms in our lives.

Multiplication Examined

"And the Earth brought forth grass, the herb that yields seed according to its kind, and the tree that yields fruit, whose seed is in itself according to its kind. And God saw that it was good." (Genesis 1:12)

We produce what we are! The church will remain weak as long as we keep producing more of the same. We need a change of mindset, attitude and motivation. In Egypt, the Israelites multiplied regardless of repression and difficulties. Many of us have strongholds (wrong ways of thinking) within us. A stronghold is a place of refuge for the enemy in the way we think. Ed Silvoso defined it like this: "A stronghold is a mindset impregnated with hopelessness which causes us to accept as unchangeable something that we know is contrary to the Word of God".

Can you identify strongholds in yourself?

"I'll never be healed"
"I'll never be out of debt"
"I'll never be an effective witness or disciple maker".
"I'll never change"

Do any of these sound familiar? However, the Bible refutes these things when it says: *"For though we walk in the flesh, we do not walk according to the flesh. For the weapons of our warfare are not carnal but mighty in God for pulling down strongholds, casting down arguments and every high thing that exalts itself against the knowledge of God, bringing every thought into captivity to the obedience of Christ, and being ready to punish all disobedience when your obedience is fulfilled."* (2 Corinthians 10:3-6)

We need to understand that there is a war going on and we have to be relentless and merciless on those things that would hinder and try to defeat us. God removes limitations!

"He sent from above, He took me; He drew me out of many waters. He delivered me from my strong enemy, from those who hated me, for they were too strong for me. They confronted me in the day of my calamity, But the Lord was my support. He also brought me out into a broad place; He delivered me because He delighted in me." (Psalms 18:16-19).

And with reference to multiplication, God says:

"Thus says the Lord: "Behold, I will bring back the captivity of Jacob's tents, and have mercy on his dwelling places; the city shall be built upon its own mound, and the palace shall remain according to its own plan. Then out of

them shall proceed thanksgiving and the voice of those who make merry; I will multiply them, and they shall not diminish; I will also glorify them, and they shall not be small. Their children also shall be as before, and their congregation shall be established before Me; and I will punish all who oppress them."" (Jeremiah 30:18-20)

And finally Ezekiel 37:26 adds:

"Moreover I will make a covenant of peace with them, and it shall be an everlasting covenant with them; I will establish them and multiply them, and I will set My sanctuary in their midst forever-more."

Authority Examined

In the Scriptures we see that, early in history, Satan rebelled against God's authority and became the 'lawless one'. On the other hand; Jesus, the only begotten Son of God, remained under authority. Because He was in submission, He was highly exalted and given a name that is above every other name. As a result of this submission Jesus was later able to say, *"All authority in Heaven and on Earth has been given to me"* (Matthew 28:18). Submission is regarded as a highly suspicious word in the church (especially in the West), but, in Luke 7:30, Jesus makes the point that the Scribes and Pharisees rejected the will of God for their lives because they were not prepared to submit to the ministry of John the Baptist.

In Psalm 40:8 the psalmist says to God, *"I delight to do your will"*. On a number of occasions, Jesus said that he had come to do the will of the Father. In the Garden of Gethsemane he spoke the famous words, "Not my will but yours be done". Jesus was a man under authority and thus he had authority. People said of him, "never a man spoke like this man. He speaks as one who has authority." Similarly, in Matthew 8, we see a Roman centurion with an understanding of authority. He knew that, in order to have authority, he needed to be under authority. Finally, in Hebrews 10:5-7 we read, *"Therefore, when Christ came into the World, he said: "Sacrifice and offering you did not desire, but a body you prepared for me; with burnt offerings and sin offerings you were not pleased. Then I said, 'Here I am—it is written about me in the scroll - I have come to do your will, my God.'"*

Where is that body now? It is the Church!

Now, there is a great difference between authority and power. A Rugby forward has power, but the referee has authority. We understand that Satan has power, but we have authority. In Genesis 1:26, we saw earlier that God gave man dominion (authority) and in Psalm 8 we read *"You have made him (man) to have dominion over the works of your hands"*.

Satan gained dominion from man by getting him to disobey God and obey him instead. However, he lost his place when Jesus died on the cross and rose from the dead, so he looked to regain it. We see in the forty days in the wilderness that Jesus didn't fall for the same trick as Adam when Satan offers Him all the kingdoms of the world. These kingdoms were

Satan's to give because he got the authority from Adam. Jesus could have thought He could go for the shortcut, but no, he did it God's way! All Satan wanted was for Jesus to worship him and he could have given the kingdoms to him, but Jesus knew that the worshipper is always subservient to the one who is worshipped. Worship is important as it is an act of submission.

In Hebrews 3:6, we see that Jesus won back that authority God's way: *"But Christ is faithful as the Son over God's house. And we are his house, if indeed we hold firmly to our confidence and the hope in which we glory."* He became obedient to the cross (Philippians 2:5-11), won back authority legally, and immediately gave it away. To whom? To the one who lost it in the first place - Man! Thus, He restored the right order as God had always intended from the beginning. Satan inspires strongholds in people in order to disable them so that they cannot operate in the authority that Jesus has restored to us.

Now, we must understand that authority operates out of holiness and truth. When we choose holiness, we are exercising authority. We say 'no' to sin and 'yes' to God. The Bible says that when we submit to God the devil flees. When we speak (preach, testify, witness, worship), we are exercising authority. However, we only have authority when we speak Kingdom truth. As soon as we speak out of our own thoughts, we lose authority just like an ambassador who fails to present the policies of the government he represents. We become an ambassador without portfolio. But every time we see someone saved, restored, discipled, healed or delivered, we are exercising Kingdom authority or dominion. We are taking ground from the enemy an enforcing Jesus' victory and rule. In Luke 10:17-19 *"The seventy-two returned with joy and said, "Lord, even the demons submit to us in your name." He replied, "I saw Satan fall like lightning from heaven. I have given you authority to trample on snakes and scorpions and to overcome all the power of the enemy; nothing will harm you.""* This is authority and the Great Commission is one of authority to "make disciples of all nations".

Keys to Fruitfulness and Multiplication

As we have already seen, we inherently have the DNA to be fruitful, to multiply, and to exercise authority or dominion. However, do we really believe that? Faith, or should I say lack of faith, is an obstacle, and since the Scriptures tell us that the work of God is to believe, we have to get into the same Scriptures to develop that faith.

The first key is abiding: The Bible says that fruitfulness comes with abiding. In John 15:5, Jesus says, *"I am the vine, you are the branches. He who abides in Me, and I in him, bears much fruit; for without Me you can do nothing."*

But how does one abide or remain in Christ? Here are four thoughts:

1. Prayer: Abiding (remaining) means being completely dependent on God and this will reveal itself in our prayer life. Our levels of prayer reveal our level of dependency. Lack of prayer often indicates that we think we can 'do life' ourselves. Prayer is the foundation of a personal time with God and regular times of prayer are important. It goes beyond just asking and puts us into a position of hearing from God.

2. Lifestyle choices: Proverbs 27:17 reveals that *"As iron sharpens iron, so one man sharpens another"*. The company we keep is an important choice. Another important choice is what we choose to do in our 'down time'. 2 Timothy 2:4 warns: *"No-one serving as a soldier gets involved in civilian affairs - he wants to please his commanding officer"*. The way we order our time shows our priorities and, like an electric plug, it is important to keep the connection clean. Holiness and separation are important because defilement leads to a bad connection.

3. Being before doing: Abiding means putting your relationship with Jesus before work for Jesus. The temptation is to work hard when loads are great, but we really need time to soak in God and have regular check-ups to ensure that our relationship is not slipping.

4. The Holy Spirit: Abiding means that we develop a personal relationship with the Holy Spirit. We need to see him as our personal pastor. Such a relationship will cause us to grow in spiritual sensitivity.

<u>The second key is sowing:</u> Fruitfulness and multiplication are only ours if we sow. Psalm 126:5-

6 says *"Those who sow in tears shall reap in joy. He who continually goes forth weeping, bearing seed for sowing, shall doubtless come again with rejoicing, bringing his sheaves with him."* Having said that 'being' must come before 'doing', it is still true that God rewards diligence and hard work. Sowing is a discipline and, very often, we can sow in one area and reap in quite another.

The third key is winning authority: Fruitfulness and multiplication are tied to winning authority. The personal battle must be won. Romans 7:14-25 talks about the inner conflict in the area of personal sins. There is also the problem of our reaction from woundedness. We need a healed heart and to be living in personal liberty. Paul asks: *"Who will rescue me from this body of death?"* (Verse 24), and then in verse 28 he gives the answer: *"Thanks be to God through Jesus Christ our Lord!"* A great example of this is found in the life of Peter who had denied knowing Jesus three times whilst standing by a fire in the courtyard of the High Priest. In John 21, again standing by a fire but this time on a beach, Jesus asks him three times: *"Do you love me?"* After he brings healing from his sin and woundedness, Jesus re-commissions Peter and tells him to *"Feed my Sheep"*.

The fourth key is relationship: Fruitfulness, multiplication and authority come to those who are in relationship. Two is better than one…one man can chase a thousand, but two men can chase ten thousand. We need to invest in people and be invested in in turn. We need cover, accountability, encouragement, correction and, in short, discipling. We all need to be discipled and to be discipling others. So, now let us turn our attention to the principles of making disciples…

PART TWO: PRINCIPLES OF DISCIPLEMAKING

Chapter 9: What is a Disciple? What is Discipleship?

A disciple is someone that Jesus has called to follow him and therefore must be considered as an 'action' term, not merely a 'thinking' term. A follower will have mission in their DNA because Jesus said of his disciples that, if they followed him, he would make them fishers of men. As a follower, everything about Jesus - his teaching, compassion and wisdom; his life, death and resurrection; his power, authority and calling - would shape every aspect of the rest of their lives. What began as simple obedience to the call of Jesus ended up changing their lives and, ultimately, the World!

The word 'disciple' (the Greek term is 'mathetes') refers to a learner, student or apprentice and discipleship in Jesus' day would involve disciples (or the Hebrew term 'talmidim') following their rabbi. Basically, a disciple is an apprentice who would go everywhere their rabbi went and <u>do</u> everything their rabbi <u>did</u>. It is impossible to be a disciple or follower of someone and not end up like that person. Jesus said, *"The student is not above the teacher, but everyone who is fully trained will be like their teacher"*. (Luke 6:40).

The concept of being a disciple is not difficult to understand, but it affects everything. In terms of the

Kingdom context, we might say that discipleship is really 'training for reigning' until we receive the spirit of adoption (Ephesians 1:5) and fulfil *"the earnest expectation of the creation"* as it *"eagerly awaits for the revealing of the sons of God"* (Romans 8:19). This revealing will take place once we have learned to think, speak and act like our Father, just as Jesus did.

Now, here's the crucial point: The disciples knew that Jesus was the master, and they knew that they were the apprentices. They knew who was who. Jesus didn't just happen to be spending a little more time with them than with others. That was the key. A disciple must know that he is a disciple of the Lord Jesus Christ, and he must understand that his role as a disciple is to become more Christ-like in every way - thought, word and deed!

People don't just happen to become disciples. It must be very intentional. A disciple must understand (because the discipler has discussed it personally and intentionally) that the discipler wants to take him to a deeper level and that he is willing to give him special attention and instruction. The disciple must willingly and eagerly accept the biblical model of the master-apprentice relationship and should feel that he's being personally invested in and is part of a team, doing something of eternal significance, something that with time and training he can model for others.

So, discipleship is when a follower of Jesus is actively helping someone else follow Jesus. Discipleship is Word-centred in that the Bible is the major focus. It is also authentic in the sense that it requires openness, honesty and transparent accountability. Thirdly, it is about reproduction, since Jesus sent his disciples out to make more disciples.

However, we often miss the trees for the wood. Too many churches are so focussed on the macro level (wood) - reaching their communities and the world with the gospel of salvation - that they miss the immense importance that the Lord places on the micro level, on how to care for and nurture individual 'trees' until they truly bear fruit that will last. Actually, the latter will accomplish the former. The few will reach the multitudes.

The Church often invests its time and energy in many worthy activities in its quest to serve the Lord. We engage in evangelism, church growth, good preaching, helpful programmes, carefully prepared worship services, imaginative youth and kids' ministry and, of course, buildings. However, there is a goal that is often talked about but not accomplished enough — that of making disciples.

I suppose the $64,000 question is, "Why aren't we doing better at making disciples?" There can be many reasons for this but some of the main reasons I can think of are as follows:

- It requires massive investment of time and openness of relationship.

- We have come to believe that what matters is that someone has made some kind of 'decision', almost as an 'end point' or 'goal'.
- We have delegated discipling to the 'paid professional'.
- We think that teaching and preaching is enough and that knowledge is the most important thing.

In a recent survey of North American evangelicals, the results showed that 97% of all those questioned had never led anyone to Christ or attempted to disciple another person. It is a fact that many, if not most, Christians do not consider themselves to be able to lead another person into a discipling relationship. I believe that this is what Jesus was alluding to when he said, "The harvest is plentiful but the workers are few." (Matthew 9:37).

Chapter 10: Making Disciples is Key

"Evangelical Christianity is now tragically below the New Testament standard. Worldliness is an accepted fact of our way of life. Our religious mood is social instead of spiritual". AW Tozer

"We must be sure to maintain the correct order of things. In Matthew 9, Jesus first forgives sins, then He healed the paralytic. In John 6:1-13 Jesus taught first and then fed the 5,000. But later in verse 26, we find that these people followed Jesus for the wrong reason. Jesus doesn't want fans, but disciples".

KP Yohannan

Instead of making disciples, we very often settle for getting decisions. We preach a message of salvation and then make an appeal which goes something like this: "Raise your hand if you want to be saved, if you want to be sure that you will go to heaven when you die". When people respond, we lead them in a short prayer of salvation whereby the respondent accepts Jesus or invites Jesus into their heart. The people are now referred to as 'saved' and may be given some literature to help them on their journey, but is this really what Jesus meant when he commanded us to 'Go and make disciples'? There is a distinction between 'decisions' and 'disciples'. We really need to understand the difference because it will impact on our practice and the way we evangelise. The gospel is not the message, but a description of the message i.e. good news; and the good news is about the arrival of the Kingdom of God, not just a salvation message. Making disciples includes salvation, of course, but it goes much further. It calls us into a learning relationship with Christ whereby we learn to think like the Father, speak like the Father, and act like the Father. Making disciples is the means by which God will get what He wants in terms of His Kingdom and His eternal purpose through the fruitfulness, multiplication and authority of His children.

Discipleship is the key to effectiveness as can be seen by the table below. However, it is not an in-house teaching programme. It is not about how much you know, but more about what you do with what you know. Our slogan must become "Every believer a disciple, every disciple a disciple-maker". The term disciple-making is misunderstood, but it really refers to the process of being apprenticed to Jesus so that He can live His life through us, His body.

Now watch what can happen if we can make true disciples in place of decisions in the chart on the next page. In the left hand column, we see what an evangelist who gets one decision every day accomplishes. In the right hand column we see what can be achieved by making disciples, where a year is spent in a discipling relationship that leads to the disciple doing the same thing to someone else. At first the evangelist appears to be most successful, but as time passes, the disciple maker overtakes him because he has understood that multiplication is far more effective in the long run than addition.

YEAR	EVANGELIST	DISCIPLE MAKER
1	365	2
2	730	4
3	1,095	8
4	1,460	16
5	1,825	32
6	2,190	64
7	2,555	128
8	2,920	256
9	3,285	512
10	3,650	1,024
15	5,475	32,768
20	7,300	1,045,696
25	9,125	33,462,272
30	10,950	1,070,792,704
33	12,045	4,283,170,816

I know the numbers are mind boggling, but it makes the point in a very impactful way. As the disciple-maker puts everything he has into the disciple and then the disciple goes to do the same to someone else, who in turn makes a disciple himself, then we see an amazing thing: What appears to be a ridiculously slow and laborious process at first (compared with the person who gets 365 decisions a year) soon begins to look respectable. By year 14, the disciple has overtaken the evangelist and, by year 33, there are over 4 billion disciples. Comically speaking, by year 34 there would be more disciples than people in the World and no one has made more than one disciple in any one year. That's the genius of fruitfulness, multiplication and authority!

Also, the evangelist who gets 365 'decisions' a year will almost certainly lose touch with those people and, without ongoing support and investment in them, not only will they not grow into disciple-makers, but they could simply remain fruitless.

Additionally, we must accept that if we don't make authentic disciples, then we won't produce good leaders, and if we don't produce good leaders we won't develop ministries, and if we don't develop ministries we won't plant functioning churches.

Jesus is the disciple-maker and, as such, he is the model. He spent the vast majority of his ministry with just 12 men (someone calculated it at 30,000 hours). So, we can see that discipleship is in-tensely relational. If you want good disciples, you have to be a good disciple yourself because most often people (new converts) go for the least possible commitment. They copy what they see. The answer is to create a red hot, radical discipleship culture. We have to see those who have the capacity to be like us and then spend significant time with them just like Jesus did. He chose the twelve *"that they might be with him"*. (Mark 3:14). But then what does it say? *"That he might send them out to preach, and to have power to heal the sick and to cast out demons."* You see, earlier when Jesus called them he said, *"Follow me and I will make you fishers of men"* (Mark 1:17). Je was not wanting to keep these disciples to himself. He was wanting to send them out. Proverbs 11:24-25 says, *"There is one who scatters, yet increases more; and there is one who withholds more than is right, but it leads to poverty."* We must learn to release people rather than focussing on trying to build a big church.

Jesus didn't give a Bible study on things - he modelled it. It was more like an apprenticeship than a college course, but we don't do it the Jesus way! Now, growing faith is something that can be served by others, but ultimately must be owned personally. Too many followers view discipleship as something that is done to them and for them, yet the writer of Hebrews made it abundantly clear that people who keep getting 'fed' in this way are in arrested development. Once out of infancy, they should no longer need to be fed, but instead be feeding others (Hebrews 5:11-13). Making disciples is active, not passive.

Even more disquieting is how we have missed out on what it is we should focus on learning. The second half of the Great Commission exhorts us to teach new believers to obey what Christ has commanded. And what has Christ commanded? Answer: To live our lives in mission to the least and the lost. In other words, what we are to be 'learning' is increased love towards others, increased obedience to God, and increased faith for the task of serving people (self-sacrifice). We are not to be in search of a feeding station that creates a culture of dependency and endless demand for head-knowledge, but a learning environment where an active life of faith is stretched and encouraged.

The most important principle that I see in biblical discipleship is that impact happens close up. The world is not transformed by making a superficial difference in many lives, but by making a profound difference in the lives of a few. Jesus understood this. Real life-change takes place not at the macro level, but at the micro level, one on one, close up. You can impress people from a distance, but you can only impact them close up. In the West, the church has flourished when it comes to impressing people from a distance but it has failed when it comes to impacting them close up. If making disciples of all nations is not the heartbeat of our life, something is wrong, either with our understanding of Christ's Church or our willingness to walk in His way.

I am often asked, "What material do you use?" Why? Because discipleship has become synonymous with a curriculum or a programme. When you've gone through it, you have been discipled. Discipleship doesn't happen in the classroom, but out where life happens. Our challenge is to understand how it is used in Scripture.

Firstly, in the Bible we can see that a disciple is firstly a follower of Jesus Christ and, in the New Testament, the word disciple is used to refer not only to fully formed followers, but to pre-faith followers. In John 6, it was clearly used to denote a group who were not yet believers. They were seekers. In verse 60 it says that they stopped following Jesus. These weren't believers who had lost their salvation, they were pre-faith followers who stopped short of placing their trust in Him. On the other hand, the term disciple also describes a mature, Christ-like follower. So, if a disciple is a follower at any stage, then the work of disciple-making actually begins pre-conversion. Traditionally, we have called this evangelism, while only post-conversion ministry is seen as discipleship. However, if 'disciple' can be used of an unbeliever, as in John 6, then it follows that disciple-making can take place with anyone, anywhere and at any time. Look at the following diagram:

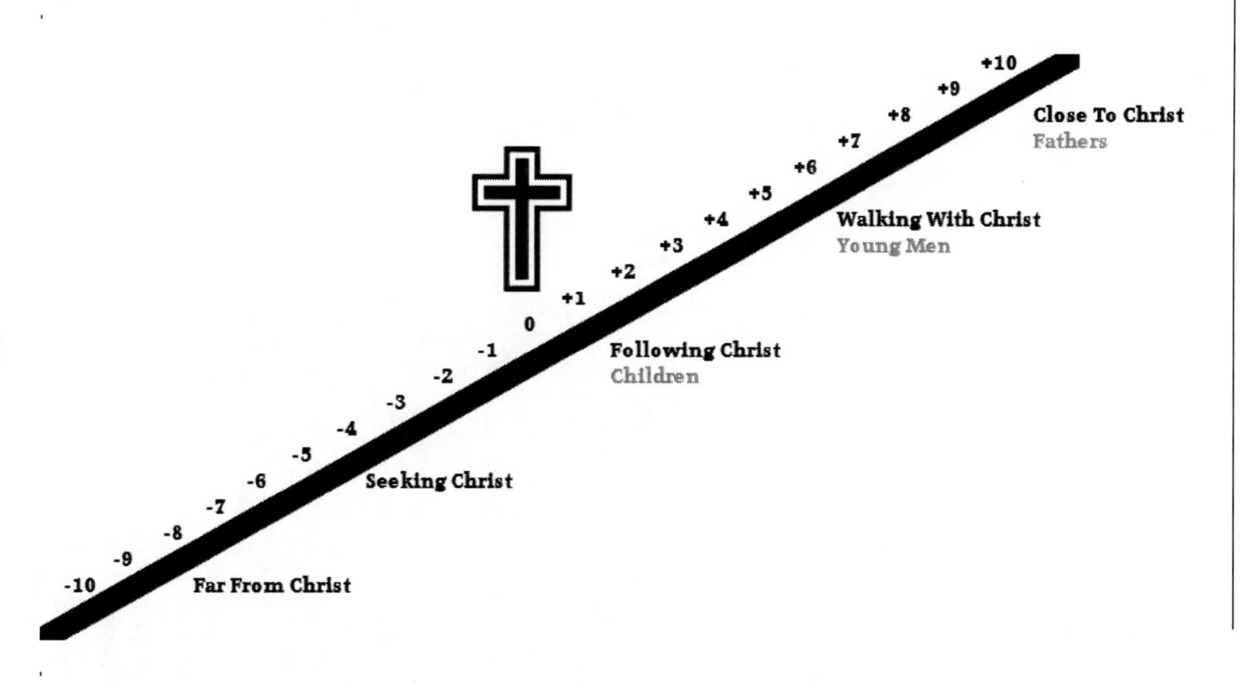
+10
+9
+8
+7
+6
+5
+4
+3
+2
+1
0
-1
-2
-3
-4
-5
-6
-7
-8
-9
-10
Close To Christ
Fathers
Walking With Christ
Young Men
Following Christ
Children
Seeking Christ
Far From Christ

We can see on the chart that discipleship may happen at any position on the continuum of minus 10 to plus 10. Our aim is to get them up the scale.

What we learn from John 6 is that our ministry to people prior to their conversion is a process and not simply an 'evangelistic event'. Unfortunately, however, evangelism has all too often been seen as just that – an event where the objective is to get a 'decision'. However, in the New Testament we do not see this at all. In fact there seemed to be little urging or coaxing or pressurising people to make a decision. Look at Peter at Pentecost, Paul and Silas with the Philippian jailer, Philip with the Ethiopian eunuch, or Peter with Cornelius: It was much more a work of the Holy Spirit. This view of discipleship helps us to see it as the life-long process of helping people move toward Jesus – toward faith and fullness in Christ. The moment of conversion is simply a very important fulcrum in the process. It's the threshold of passing from darkness to light, from death to life, but it is neither the finish line nor the starting point of the disciple-making process. Consequently, when we pray for God to provide us with people to disciple, we should ask Him for disciples on both sides of the cross.

Secondly, we can see that discipleship is a learning process. Whilst 'a follower' is the most common understanding of the word disciple, the most literal translation from the Greek (mathetes) means 'a student' or 'a learner'. A disciple is a learner, an apprentice, someone who is learning to imitate his master. I like the word 'learner' for the simple reason that it conveys the idea that it is a process.

And what are we to be learning? We should be learning to:

- **Love Like Jesus.** Not knowledge. Not a conversion experience. Not church membership. Not spiritual gifts. Not doctrinal purity. But love.
- **Lose Like Jesus.** It could mean friends, family, wealth, financial security, reputation or whatever it takes to bring glory to God and the gospel.
- **Live Like Jesus.** The Great Commission includes teaching to observe or obey. Disciples are recognised by obedience to all that Jesus commanded.

So we may define a disciple in this way:

"A disciple is one who is **learning** to **live** and **love** like Jesus and **helps others to do the same**."

Chapter 12: The Simplicity of Discipling

"When the solution is simple, God is answering."
Albert Einstein

"The spontaneous expansion of the Church reduced to its elements is a very simple thing."
Roland Allen

All reproduction begins at a molecular level, and develops from the micro to the macro, from the simple to the complex. It's the same with the Kingdom of God. In Mark 4:30-32, we read the Parable of the Mustard Seed and learn that the Kingdom of God must start at the smallest of levels and grow via multiplication to have great and expansive influence. If we cannot multiply leaders, we will never multiply churches and if we cannot multiply disciples, we will not multiply leaders. Disciples, leaders, churches - in that order.

The basic unit of Kingdom life is one follower of Christ in relationship with another follower of Christ. The micro form of church life is a unit of two or three believers in relationship. The Bible often elevates a group of two or three to significance. Both the Old and New Testaments mention the phrase 'two or three' and it is interesting that at least ten times 'two or three' is suggested as an ideal size at which to conduct ministry. I believe that 'two or three' is also an ideal number for conducting some aspects of discipling for the following reasons:

- Community is stronger with two or three (Ecclesiastes 4:9-12). Not only do they share effort and get a good return for their labour, but they can also help and encourage one another.
- Accountability is stronger (1 Timothy 5:19). According to Levitical law, no one could bring a case to trial without two or three witnesses. Paul carries the idea of accountability when dealing with sin as well.
- Confidentiality is stronger (Matthew 18:15-17). There is a balance between accountability and confidentiality. The less people know something, the greater the confidentiality and the likelihood of dealing with issues in an open and honest way.
- Flexibility is stronger (Matthew 18:20). It's is easier to get two or three together in one place at the same time than it is for a larger group.
- Communication is stronger (1 Corinthians 14:26-33). The more voices you add to an equation, the more confusion results and breakdown occurs.
- Direction is stronger (2 Corinthians 13:1). With the Corinthians, Paul used an Old Testament principle of two or three witnesses to confirm direction. The counsel of two or three may help in the case of uncertainty.
- Leadership is stronger (1 Corinthians 14:29). Paul suggests that only two or three prophetic voices should provide leadership to a spiritual community at any one time. The others are to

weigh the voices. There is wisdom in a plurality of leaders, but too many can also be a problem – leadership by committee can be a barrier to progress, and we've all heard the phrase 'too many chiefs, and not enough Indians'. If the children of Israel had been led by a committee (12 spies), they would still be in Egypt. Two or three is safer than a solo leader, yet more powerful than a committee.

- Reproduction is easier at this level also. If you have a group of three and you want to multiply it, all you have to do is find one more person. By reducing multiplication to this simplest level, reproduction can be a part of the genetic fabric (DNA) of the entire body of Christ.

Reproduction always occurs at the microscopic level - even in our own bodies, right now! Multiplication of cells will continue until we die. Without cells multiplying, the body will die. Multiplication stops when death occurs, but equally death occurs when multiplication stops. It may sound paradoxical, but there is also a spiritual truth that multiplication also starts with death. There is a cost involved in multiplication. With salmon (and many examples in the insect kingdom), for example, the cost of reproducing is death. In John 12:24 Jesus said, *"Very truly I tell you, unless a kernel of wheat falls to the ground and dies, it remains only a single seed. But if it dies, it produces many seeds."*

As disciples, Jesus said we must deny ourselves and pick up our cross to follow him. This is all about surrender. This is about confession and repentance. This is about obedience. Where these things exist, there is a death, a dying to self, and growth and reproduction or multiplication will result. We have got to be willing to give up more than just our time, talents and treasure; we've got to start giving up our lives for the sake of King Jesus and his kingdom. If we are willing to pay the price - if we are willing to die to follow Christ - then we will see an abundant harvest of souls for the Kingdom of God. This is how the 1st Century believers were able to reach the whole of their world at that time with the Gospel of the Kingdom within one generation, even without all the modern methods of communication we have today.

I have heard it said that scientific and statistical probabilities demonstrate that if a single shaft of wheat is left undamaged and allowed to freely reproduce and grow, it multiplies into a crop large enough to feed the entire world population for an entire year within only eight years. It takes only one apple seed to grow a tree, yet a single apple tree produces enough seed to plant an entire or-chard. Multiplication must start small and seemingly insignificant, but with time and generational reproduction, it reaches a global level of influence.

Remember the multiplication table back in chapter 10? What if all of us decided to put everything else aside and focus on truly discipling another for just the next few years in a manner that multiplies? We could conceivably finish the Great Commission in just a few years.

On the reverse side, of course, we must understand that Christianity is just one generation away from extinction. If we fail to reproduce ourselves and pass the torch of life into the hands of the next generation, the church will be over within just one generation. Yet, because of the power of multiplication, we are also only one generation away from the worldwide fulfilment of the Great Commission. The choice is ours. What are we waiting for?

No wonder the apostle Peter said that we should be:

"Looking for and hastening the coming day of God" 2 Peter 3:12.

Chapter 13: The Basics of Discipling

There are three searching questions that I ask myself in order to establish if discipling is taking place in my own life. Firstly, "Who is investing in my life?" In order to be a lifelong learner I need people investing into my life. In order to make a disciple I first have to be one. This kind of relation-ship causes me to grow and, as I abide in Christ, produce fruit that will lead to multiplication.

This leads to a second question: "Whose life am I investing in?" One cannot be a disciple without making one also. We cannot say that we are following Christ without doing what he says. This leads to the third question, "What is God saying to me and what am I doing about it?"

We see this principle espoused by Paul in 2 Timothy 2:2 *"And the things you have heard me say in the presence of many witnesses entrust to reliable people who will also be qualified to teach others."* Here we see three generations: Paul to Timothy; Timothy to reliable people; reliable people to others. There is of course the expectation that the 'others' will also pass it on.

Next, we must come to see that biblical discipleship is not a curriculum or a programme. It is highly relational and more about doing life together than attending meetings. Of course teaching of the Bible is extremely important (although teaching people how to read the Bible for themselves, for all its worth, is even more important), but Jesus' approach was much more than that. His style was much more like an apprenticeship. Of course the modern-day apprentice gets 'day release' to attend college and study, but by far the greatest part is the daily practical teaching 'on the job'. The other principle I see in Jesus' approach is that of immersion. If Jesus spent up to 30,000 hours in total with his disciples, then we have to start thinking in terms of a greater immersion into discipleship than we currently practice.

Whilst a teacher is involved in the discipleship process, we have to try to understand what Jesus meant by his command to make disciples. If you notice, our modern understanding puts the entire emphasis on someone or something 'doing' discipleship 'to' someone else. The one being discipled is seemingly passive - in other words discipleship is something to be 'received'. But that is not the idea of discipleship in the Bible. Whilst it is true that it contains the idea of following (specifically Jesus), the word disciple is from the Greek word 'mathetes' and literally means 'learner'. Think about it. If I'm not mistaken, that puts the action firmly into the lap of the one doing the learning.

Jesus was teaching, but he fulfilled the teaching/ equipping role by inviting 12 men (and more than a few women) to do life with him for three years. They were called disciples, but as we reflect on those early followers we can see that theirs was an invitation to learn, not to enter into a passive process of being 'fed'. If discipleship was something that was done to someone, then Jesus failed in epic proportions when it comes to Judas Iscariot! I wonder if Judas ever complained of 'not being fed'?

So what would that kind of discipleship look like? What might it entail? Different people (I will examine some later) have come up with different ways of engaging with discipleship but they all have some commonality. In his book 'Deep and Wide', Andy Stanley states the practice of many seasoned spiritual leaders in detailing the five primary ways people experience growth in their faith:

1. Practical Teaching - it's not about how much we know, but what we **DO** with what we know.
2. Private Disciplines - fruitfulness is all about abiding in Christ through spiritual disciplines.
3. Personal Ministry - becoming actively involved as participants, not just spectators.
4. Providential Relationships - where iron sharpens iron.
5. Pivotal Circumstances - situations that God allows in order for us to grow as we embrace them.

Summing up then, we can say that discipleship is key. Making disciples was a command, not a request. It happens close-up. Its final goal is God's threefold blessing and destiny for His children: Fruitfulness, multiplication and authority. This is God's way of getting what He wants - a family, a house, a body for Christ and a Bride for His Son for 'the age to

come'. It is God's way of getting a people who think like him, speak like him and act like him.

PART THREE: PRACTICAL DISCIPLEMAKING AND PERSONAL EXPERIENCES

Chapter 14: How to Find a Disciple and What to Look For

Referring back to the diagram in chapter 11 showing the -10 to +10 continuum, we see people on either side of the cross. Traditionally, we have only considered people for discipleship on the 'born again' side of the cross. Of course, believers at all stages of maturity need discipling and I believe that everyone should have a fellow believer investing in their life whilst also investing in the life of a less mature Christ follower. However, it is also incredibly important to be discipling a non-believer to conversion. Easier said than done?

I recently came across an acrostic which I feel really helps us practically to understand how we might find someone to disciple to conversion. It is an acrostic on the word 'B.L.E.S.S'. This reduces what is often seen as a very difficult task to easy steps that, I believe, everybody can attempt:

B	**Begin with Prayer.** This is crucial. We all know it, but do we really do it? Pray and ask the Holy Spirit to lead you to a 'person of peace' that will be open to what you have to say. (We will look at the 'person of peace' very shortly, but basically it refers to a person who is open to what we have to say).
L	**Listen**. We must actively look for a disciple. Who should we be looking for? It is only by listening that we will find out if someone is a 'person of peace'.
E	**Eat.** This was a big thing in the Bible and in many cultures today. This is where relationships begin to develop. Invite someone for a coffee or to your home for a meal
S	**Serve.** This is where self-sacrifice is called for. People know when we're authentic. Be prepared to be transparent, loving, and giving (time and self).
S	**Story.** You have a story. God has a story. Put together and practise sharing your testimony. Be equipped to share the good news of the Kingdom with others where possible.

Now, when it comes to people who have already made a 'decision for Christ' but have not really entered into the discipling process, we can use another acrostic to help us find the person that the Lord would have us share our lives with. Personally, I try to find F.A.T people! If I am going to be investing a great deal of time and energy into a person I would like to know that it is going to be a fruitful relationship. I don't have time to waste on, well, time-wasters! A F.A.T. person is one who is

Faithful, Available and Teachable and, as I consider specific people to disciple and wait on the Lord for guidance, there are certain things that I look for and ask God about.

Faithful people are people who do what they say they are going to do. In Matthew chapter 25, we read the parable of the talents where we see that God is looking for people with the humility to do small things and trustworthiness to do them well. I ask myself a few things about the person I am considering: Are they consistent and punctual? Can they be relied upon to do what is asked of them and do it well? Do they give up at the first sign of difficulty? Are they the 'go the extra mile' kind of person? Do they return phone calls, emails and invitations promptly? Do they respond to various requests for help?

Available people are identified by their internal motivation to serve the Lord. At a basic level, of course, a person must literally be available and internally motivated to carve out time to meet. It makes no sense, and does no good, to force or prod or even have to coax someone to be a disciple. Feed sheep, don't chase goats! In Isaiah 6:8, we see the correct response, *"Here am I, send me!"* Again, I ask myself some questions about the person I am considering: Are they active or passive? Do they read? Do they seek out opportunities to grow? Do they pray for opportunities to serve? To witness? Are they interested in going with me to learn? Are they interested in short-term missions? Do they give? Do they initiate relationships? Do they read the Bible and pray?

Teachable people have a willingness to learn and put into practice what they learn. Always remember that it is not about how much a person knows, but what they do with what they know! This is arguably the most important characteristic in the context of discipleship because it will determine whether you have any chance of being effective in helping that person to grow and mature in their faith to the point of being able to spiritually reproduce in the lives of others. Two primary, repetitive questions are: 'What has the Lord said to you?' and 'What are you doing about it?' For example, if you explain the scriptural importance of being baptised, does the person show an eagerness to be baptised? If you explain the Bible's emphasis on developing a disciplined prayer life (and model it), does the person imitate? The bottom line is this: Does the person seem willing to practice what is preached?

All of us have a learning curve of course. We don't all start off two thirds the way up the ladder. We are not looking for perfect people. Rest assured, they won't be! What you are looking for here is potential. As you begin to try to make disciples who make disciples, you might be surprised, even discouraged, by how few people in the world (even in church) really have teachable hearts and spirits. Don't be. Remember, the road to abundant, eternal life is narrow indeed. That's just the way it is. Secondly, and even more important, rather than being discouraged, be determined to find 'faithful men' who will be qualified not just to learn from you but to 'teach others also'. You are not looking for many, but for a few who will benefit enormously from your investment in them. There-fore, rather than having soaring expectations built on quantity, have specific expectations built on quality. The parable of the seed and the sower in Matthew 13:3-8 and 18-23 shows us that many who receive the good news with joy at first, fail to produce fruit. Interestingly, people with a lot of issues in their lives can make great disciples - lots of manure makes for fertile soil.

Not every heart is a willing heart. Not every heart is fertile soil, but we shouldn't be discouraged. The Lord is looking for, in movie parlance, 'a few good men' (and women) in whose lives you can invest and, as we saw in the multiplication table earlier, the returns on the investment will astound you. Yes, there will be failures and casualties - even Jesus had a Judas! But keep in mind that the people who will most likely respond favourably to your discipleship will be people who are faithful, available and teachable.

Now, returning to people who are not yet believers, let us look at what we mean by finding the 'person of peace'. In Luke 10:1-12, we see Jesus' evangelistic strategy. He told his disciples that the harvest was plentiful and sent them out, not with a combative message but with a message of peace. If the people they spoke to accepted the peace, then the disciples would invest time into that person. If the people approached weren't interested in the message, then Jesus told his disciples to just move on. The key that unlocks the process is the 'person of peace', the person that is open to hearing what God will give you to say at that moment. We need to keep our eyes open looking out for the people of peace that are in our lives. For that we need perception. Perception is like 'testing the temperature' to see if someone is a person of peace.

The thing that I notice is that we are not expected to declare our message to people who are antagonistic toward us. Many people fear evangelism because they have been told that they must preach the gospel to everybody whether they are interested or not. No-one likes being ridiculed or rejected. Trust me, that will happen often enough in life without going looking for it! No, the apostle Peter exhorts us to *"Always be prepared to give an answer to everyone who asks you to give the reason for the hope that you have. But do this with gentleness and respect"* (1 Peter 3:15).

Chapter 15: Practical: How to Make a Disciple and What to Do

It seems to me that there is no 'one size fits all' approach to making disciples. The principles may remain the same, but like any artisan, we need a number of tools in our toolkit. The key will be finding the right tool for the job in hand.

Referring back to the diagram in chapter 11 regarding the -10 to +10 continuum, I have used some categories that have been espoused by Willow Creek Church in Chicago. There is some biblical support for such an approach, since the apostle John uses his own categories in chapter two of his first epistle where he refers to 'little children', 'young men' and 'fathers'. In their 'Reveal Studies', the Willow Creek Church use categories to describe people's spiritual state. They are 'far from Christ', 'seeking Christ', 'exploring Christ', 'growing in Christ', 'close to Christ', and 'Christ-centred'.

The key thing is to try to discern where a potential disciple is up to and select the right tool for the job. Discover where a person is up to on the scale by listening carefully to them and then select your strategy accordingly. Each of the following tools that I use myself will be explained in more detail later, but as a simple guide I recommend the following strategies:

- With those who are ‘far from Christ’, use Discovery Bible Study (DBS)
- With those ‘seeking Christ’, use DBS or invite to an Alpha Course
- With those ‘exploring Christ’, use DBS, Alpha or Multiply.
- With those ‘growing in Christ’, use Life Transformation Groups (LTGs), ABC Groups, or Multiply.
- With those ‘close to Christ’ use LTGs, ABC Groups, LifeShapes and a mentoring relationship.
- With those who are Christ-centred use LifeShapes and spiritual friendships.

It is always important to remember that these strategies must be seen not as programmes or curricula, but as tools to be used within the context of a close discipling relationship. The tools are there to serve you! Use them wisely to suit the situation, not as a rigid programme or curriculum. The most important thing here is relationship.

Leadership Requirements: It is also important to note that some tools have greater leadership requirements than others. The greater the leadership requirement, the less reproducible the group is. LifeShapes and Alpha groups require experienced and trained leadership, as does a mentoring relationship. Multiply and DBS only require a leader in the case of group application (as opposed to one-to-one). Spiritual friendships, LTGs and ABC Groups do not require a recognised leader, mainly because they are groups of two or three.

Describing Alpha, Mentoring, and Spiritual Friendships is really beyond the scope of this book. Briefly, the **Alpha Course**, now known simply as **Alpha**, is an evangelistic course which seeks to introduce the basics of the Christian faith through a series of talks and discussions. It is described by its organisers as "an opportunity to explore the meaning of life". Alpha courses are being run in churches, homes, workplaces, prisons, universities and a wide variety of other locations. The course is being run around the world by all major Christian denominations.

A mentoring relationship may be described as one where an experienced and trusted adviser or guide develops another person to achieve defined spiritual goals. It is most common in leadership circles. On the other hand, Spiritual Friendships tend to be between two peers that have come to a place where they realise they need to have someone in their life who can encourage them, speak into their world, ask the hard questions, and hold them accountable. It tends to be a mutual arrangement, and often quite informal.

Before going on to discuss other strategies in more detail in the later chapters of this book, let us just remind ourselves of the kind of things that a disciple needs to learn. Whilst it is true that disciple making is not a curriculum or programme, there are certain things a disciple needs to learn in a practical way.

Here are some skills that we all need but many fail to acquire:

- How to read the Bible and interpret it properly (hermeneutics).
- How to pray and develop in other spiritual disciplines.
- How to get spiritual breakthrough to become more Christlike.
- How to develop deeper relationships in every sphere of life.
- How to find right balances and rhythms in life.
- How to multiply.
- How to determine personal calling.
- How to maintain spiritual health.
- How to engage in relational mission.
- How to hear from God.

There is a big difference in giving people some information that leads to education and teaching people how to do something that will lead to transformation. However, when we teach people how to do something, there needs to be some accountability in order to assure that what is being learned is also being put into practice. Again I say, it is not how much one knows but what one does with what one knows. That is the litmus test of the discipling process, and it is within intentional relationships that accountability happens best.

Chapter 16: Discovery Bible Studies

The Discovery Bible Study (DBS) is a very useful tool that helps equip every believer for the joy of Bible-centred disciple making. This approach, as its name suggests, is a method of helping people to discover Christ for themselves through the Bible. It can be used with the person of peace who may be far from Christ, seeking Christ or exploring Christ. I have used DBS with people from each of these categories with great success. The first two studies examine the Creation Story; the next three explore what the Bible has to say about the Fall; and the rest the address issue of Redemption. DBS can go on for as long as one desires, but done once a week, it can go on for 6 months (a far cry from a 10 minute presentation followed by an attempt to 'close the deal'). Ideally a group would consist of 1-5 other people and last for about an hour, during which four sections would be covered: Opening, Review, Passage, and Application. There now follows a guideline for a small group 'Discovery Bible Study':

OPENING: When you meet with your group (1-5 other people) for DBS, have each one **share one thing they are thankful for and one thing that is a concern or that they are struggling with.** Then enter into a time of group prayer based on the joys and concerns that were shared.

REVIEW: Beginning at the second meeting, review the past week. Ask each one to share if and **what**

God has shown them in their personal time with him since your last meeting. Then ask how they are doing with obeying the things the Lord pointed out to them in the last session. This is one thing that sets DBS apart from most discipleship tools - it is OBEDIENCE oriented! *"Teaching them to obey everything I have commanded you"* (Matthew 28:20).

PASSAGE: This section amounts to an 'inductive' study approach i.e. Observation followed by questions for Interpretation and Application.

'Observation' is accomplished in the reading and retelling of the passage. Have someone read the passage (passages listed at the end of this chapter) **out loud** while everyone follows in his or her Bible. **When they have finished, ask for a volunteer to retell the passage in their own words** (without looking at the Bible and without giving personal commentary). **When they finish, ask the group to fill in any points they feel were omitted. Next, ask for another volunteer to retell the passage again in their own words, hopefully filling in any holes in the story.** Reading, listening, and retelling Scripture is more important that you might think. This pattern allows different learning styles to engage Scripture. Everyone has time to think about the passage and allows the Holy Spirit to speak through God's Word. Allowing the group to add to the retelling encourages everyone to think about and retain the main points in the passage. We call this part of the 'passage' section 'Observation'. Then, we move on to 'Interpretation'.

'Interpretation' is what we call discovery through questions. After the group has read and retold the Scripture, you can study the passage. **Your discussion must be question driven.** Questions facilitate the discovery process and allow the group to wrestle with Scripture and grow spiritually. Questions must be open questions (requiring more than a yes or no answer) that will encourage interaction with the Scripture. Typical questions may include: What does this passage tell us/ reveal about God? What does this passage tell us/ reveal about humanity? What in this passage caught your attention or surprised you and why? Did anything in this passage bother you and why? Are there any lessons/ principles this passage reveals about being a disciple and follower of Jesus? What is the central message of the passage? What does this passage tell us about living to honour and please God? We should do our best to keep the discussion focussed on Scripture. If you or someone else in the group is well-read, it will be hard to avoid introducing outside materials into the study. As a facilitator, you need to work hard to limit the discussion of extra-Biblical or other Biblical material. These materials can be helpful, but they don't necessarily facilitate interaction with Scripture. Many times they underscore the intelligence of the one introducing the materials rather than keeping Scripture at centre stage!

Now we move on to the final part of the passage section: 'Application'.

'Application' is about a commitment to obey the Scriptures. Knowledge of God's Word must translate into **obedience**, or it is wasted. As I have said many times before, it is not about **what you know** but **what you do with what you know!** The vital question is: **How can/will I specifically apply the teachings of this passage to the way I live my life starting immediately? What does God want me to change in my life in order to become more like Jesus?** It is important to try to be very specific in answering this question. If time allows, it will be encouraging for the group to have a few moments to share what they feel God is saying to them. If they are already obeying the major lesson in this passage of Scripture, have them share how they obey it. Encourage the group to **identify specific things** they can do to obey the passage.

Finally, ask them to consider who they are going to share this passage within the next few days!

Summary:

- Ask everyone to share one thing they are thankful for and one thing that is stressful or of concern to them and take those things to God in prayer.
- Ask the group to share what God has shown them through his Word since the last meeting. Ask them to share how they have been obedient to the previous week's Scripture and who they might have shared the story with during the last week.
- Have someone read the Scripture passage out loud while people follow along in their Bibles.

- Have someone else retell the same passage out loud while the group listens. Allow the group to add or delete any elements to the retelling, if necessary.
- Have another person in the group retell the passage again filling in anything that was left out in his or her own words.
- Use the discovery questions to encourage the group to engage in the passage.
- Challenge the group to obey God's Word. Have people write down what he or she is going to do to obey what God has shown them through the passage over the next week.
- Have the group identify a person or persons they will share the passage with during the next week.
- Close in prayer.

The beauty of DBS is that it is non-threatening. Most people don't want to come to church with you and most people don't want to hear your opinions about Christianity. Many people don't believe in the Jesus we love and they are carrying all sorts of misconceptions and emotional baggage in relation to the church and Christians. DBS can help avoid these barriers because it invites people to say what they think. DBS doesn't tell them what to think or believe, it merely exposes them to the Word of God - and that is enough!

DBS trusts in the power of the Word of God and the Holy Spirit. It trusts in the power of self-discovery. It provides a mutual learning experience and is easily reproducible - almost anyone can do it!

LIST OF DISCOVERY BIBLE STUDIES

Scripture	Discussion Topic
Genesis 1:1-25	The Creation Story: God Created the World
Genesis 2:4-24	The Creation Story: The Creation of Man
Genesis 3:1-13	The Fall: The First Sin and Judgment
Genesis 3:14-24	The Fall: Judgment of a Sinful World
Genesis 6:1-9-17	The Fall: The Flood
Genesis 12:1-8; 15:1-6	Redemption: God's Promise to Abraham
Genesis 22:1-19	Redemption: Abraham Offers Isaac as a Sacrifice
Exodus 12:1-28	Redemption: The Promise of Passover
Exodus 20:1-21	Redemption: The Ten Commandments
Leviticus 4:1-25	Redemption: The Sacrificial System
Isaiah 53	Redemption: Isaiah Foreshadows of the Coming Promise
Luke 1:26-38; 2:1-20	Redemption: The Birth of Jesus
Matthew 3; John 1:29-34	Redemption: Jesus is Baptised
Matthew 4:1-11	Redemption: The Temptation of Christ
John 3:1-21	Redemption: Jesus and Nicodemus

John 4:1-26, 39-42	Redemption: Jesus and the Woman at the Well
Luke 5:17-26	Redemption: Jesus Forgives and Heals
Mark 4:35-41	Redemption: Jesus Calms the Storm
Mark 5:1-20	Redemption: Jesus Casts Out Evil Spirits
John 11:1-44	Redemption: Jesus Raises Lazarus from the Dead
Matthew 26:26-30	Redemption: The First Lord's Supper
John 18:1-40; 19:1-16	Redemption: Jesus is Betrayed and Condemned
Luke 23:32-56	Redemption: Jesus is Crucified
Luke 24:1-35	Redemption: Jesus Conquers Death
Luke 24:36-53	Redemption: Jesus Appears and Ascends
John 3:1-21	Redemption: We Have a Choice

Chapter 17: Life Transformation Groups and ABC Groups

Life Transformation Groups (LTGs) are a great tool to use in the disciple-making process. An LTG is made up of two or three people of the same gender, who meet weekly for personal accountability for their spiritual growth and development. It is recommended that a group not grow beyond three, but multiply into two groups of two once the fourth participant has proved faithful to the process. Firstly, they must stay faithful to the healing process. Secondly, they must stay faithful to the goals. In 2 Timothy 2:2, Paul encourages his protégé to commit the things he has seen and heard Paul demonstrate to faithful men who will in turn teach others by example.

Developed by Neil Cole and presented in his books 'Cultivating a Life for God' and 'Ordinary Hero', LTGs are a simple, yet powerful, way to reproduce disciples. Our discipleship must have no less a goal than a transformed life. Conformity to external standards is not enough. We must set hearts aflame with passion for Christ. In another of his books, 'Search and Rescue', Cole outlines the basic elements of the group using the analogy from the world of a lifeguard - cardio pulmonary resuscitation (CPR). CPR on the beach or pool consists of getting water out of the lungs (exhaling), in order to get oxygen into the lungs (inhaling), and then a return to consciousness (activity).
In the same way, spiritual CPR consists of three things - confession, Bible study and communication, as follows:

Exhaling = Confessing your sins to one another (2 Tim 2:19-21). You can't get any oxygen in until you get the water out. The difference between a vessel of honour and dishonour is that, with a vessel of dishonour, you can make deposits but you can't make withdrawals. Confession is verbal agreement - that's what police officers are looking for. Hearing confession is part of the role of priesthood (of all believers), but it must be mutual.

Inhaling = Planting of God's Word in your heart (2 Tim 3:16-17). The truth is that it's God's Word that changes lives. No amount of books, tools, or sermons can replace a steady diet of God's Word for equipping God's people.

If you want to build a new house, it is necessary to clear the plot and prepare the ground first (confession) before we can build (read Scripture). If you put on clean clothes you must first take off the dirty, smelly ones. The Bible talks of 'putting off the old and putting on the new' (Col 3:8-14; Eph 4:22-24; Rom 13:12-14; James 1:21 and 1 Pet 2:1-2). Peter agrees with Paul on the two elements needed for growth in a disciple's life: continual cleansing from sin and a steady diet of God's Word.

Activity = Communication. The third idea with which Paul concludes his letter to Timothy is related to spiritual breathing. It is the act of communicating. In a real sense, this is the great work that we are all being prepared and equipped to do (2 Tim 4:1-5). Paul concludes this passage by saying…"Do the work of sharing the good news" (my translation). Paul has repeatedly used a couple of words together to make a point. He has said that confession and cleansing ***prepares*** us for every **good work** (2 Tim 2:21) and he has said that consuming the Scriptures ***equips*** us for every **good work**. (2 Tim 3:16-17).

It is not enough to know facts about the Gospels and Epistles - we must put them into practice to fulfil the commission. Even obeying them is not enough. We do not fulfil this command until others are fulfilling it because of our influence. According to 2 Tim 2:2, success is not achieved until the 4th generation. The church is often educated beyond its obedience, and more education will not help. What we need is more obedience. As I have already said, what you do with what you know is the important thing. There is a striking similarity between the last words of Jesus and those of Paul. Each was telling their closest companions to make disciples who will make disciples - to the end of the age.

The unstoppable power of multiplication was demonstrated in the table in chapter 10. However, we choose the more immediate success and instant gratification of addition instead of waiting for the momentum where we can build through multiplication. The big test is to make every disciple a first disciple i.e. a disciple of Christ, not a disciple of us. Each one copied from the original, not from successive copies (which, as with a photocopy, become fainter and fainter).

Everyone needs backup. 2 Tim 2:22 says: *"Run away from the evil things that young people long for. Try hard to do what is right. Have faith, love and peace.* ***Do these things together with those who call on the Lord from a pure heart."*** Note the use of plural nouns in 2 Tim 2:2 - witnesses, men, others. Lives change in the context of community. The concept of a "Lone Ranger Christian" is an oxymoron!

However, there is a cost involved with multiplication. In nature we see that reproduction can often cost the life of the one reproducing, just like the salmon. Jesus said, *"Very truly I tell you, unless a grain of wheat falls to the ground and dies, it remains only a single seed. But if it dies, it produces many seeds".* The following is a true hero story told by Neil Cole in his book 'Search and Rescue' by way of illustration:

> "Liza had a serious disease which required a transfusion, and her little five year old brother was the best match. The doctors explained the situation to the little boy and asked him if he would be willing to give his blood to his sister. He hesitated for a moment, took a deep breath and said, "Yes, I'll do it if it will save Liza". As the transfusion progressed, he lay on a bed next to his sister. Everyone smiled as they saw the colour return to Liza's cheeks. But the boy's face grew pale and his smile faded. He looked up at the doctor and asked with a trembling voice, "Will I start to die straight away?" He had thought that he was going to have to give his

sister all of his blood. Real heroes come in all sizes! Jesus was also willing to give all of his blood, his life, so that we could live. How can we do anything less?"

ABC Groups are very similar to LTGs, except for the fact that they can be slightly larger, ideally 2-4 persons. I tend to work with these groups fortnightly as they alternate with the larger LifeShapes groups which we will look at in the next chapter. We call them ABC Groups because of what they accomplish: 'A' stands for accountability; 'B' stands for Bible study; and 'C' stands for commission. So, as you can see, the aims and objectives are very similar to LTGs.

Both LTGs and ABC Groups are a grassroots tool for growth. Through these simple groups, the most essential elements of vital spiritual ministry are released to common Christians without the need for specialised training. It taps the disciples' internal motivation and provides the support needed to grow in the essentials of a spiritual life. These groups empower the common Christian to do the uncommon work of reproductive discipling.

Here is a simple overview of what an LTG or ABC group is:

- They meet once a week (LTG) or once a fortnight (ABC) for approximately an hour.
- They are groups of 2-3 (LTG) or 2-4 (ABC) and additional people result in multiplication.
- The groups are not co-ed, but gender specific.

- There is no curriculum, workbook or training involved.
- There is no leader needed in the group.
- Only three tasks are accomplished (openness and honesty in mutual accountability; Scripture reading repetitively in entire context and in community; souls are prayed for strategically, specifically, and continuously).

The strengths of these groups are to be found in the level of community found in micro groups of 2, 3, or 4. Accountability is strong and confidentiality is higher. They are extremely flexible in that it is much easier to coordinate the diaries of 2-4 people, so the smaller, the better. Finally, these groups are very reproducible because of their size and because recognised leaders are not a requirement for multiplication.

In the movie 'Pay It Forward', junior high student Trevor McKinney presents an idea that he thinks will change the world. He suggests that, rather than pay people back for what they do, people do a favour that really helps someone and tell that person not to pay it back, but to pay it forward to three other people who, in turn, each pay it forward to three more - and on and on into a global outpouring of kindness and decency.

Disciple-making has an even greater potential to change the world if Christians will just pay it forward! As they learn and grow through the input of spiritual nurturing and encouragement, they need to pass it on to someone else who will, in turn, pay it forward to someone else. As each person continues this process over and over again, it will have a lasting impact on our church and community.

Chapter 18: LifeShapes and Spiritual Growth

Sociologists tell us that language creates culture. A common language is often the most obvious outward sign that people share a common culture. For this reason, groups seeking to mobilise their members often insist on their own distinct language. There are things in language that influence how its speakers see reality. Concepts are developed through language, not the other way round, and this is why such emphasis is placed on language development in the education system. If we want to create a culture of discipleship, we need a language to support it. Success in discipling people depends largely on having an agreed-on language.

The language that Mike Breen developed for this is called LifeShapes - it is a collection of eight shapes, and each shape represents a foundational teaching of Jesus or a principle from His life. How have we shifted from talking about language to talking about shapes? Well, Breen says that images and symbols are effective as a language because one image can convey a lot of things. If you've ever heard the old saying 'a picture paints a thousand words', then you'll understand how imagery can convey a message simply and succinctly. Jesus lived in an oral culture which gave way to a written culture. Today, however, we have entered into an image-based culture where huge amounts of information, stories and data are attached to images. Our brains are literally wired differently than they were a hundred years ago, and so Mike Breen reasons that the idea of attaching the teachings of Jesus and Scripture to a few basic images is perfectly in line with how our brains are already hardwired.

Mike Breen declares that, after a year in a discipling relationship in a group, this is what we'd want people to know, and this is what we'd want people to be able to experience:

- They should be seeing continual spiritual breakthrough. This is about learning to always listen to the voice of God and respond. This is represented by **'The Circle'**, which is the foundational shape and one every group returns to as we continually ask, "What is God saying to me, and what am I going to do about it?"
- Disciples should develop healthy rhythms of life. We learn to develop a rhythm of rest and work daily, weekly, and annually. This means learning to pray and read Scripture every day in a meaningful way. Building Sabbath into our week, month and seasons recreates us. We also learn how to develop other individual and corporate spiritual disciplines in our lives. This is represented by **The Semi-Circle.**
- **The Triangle** conveys how we develop deeper and balanced relationships. We learn to live in deeper relationships that are balanced between our life with God (up), our life within the church (in) and our life with people who don't know Jesus yet (out).
- Everyone must engage in multiplying disciples. **The Square** is the shape that helps us to learn the process Jesus used for discipling people. We

discover where we ourselves are in that four-stage process, and how to begin looking toward discipling people ourselves.

- **The Pentagon** concerns personal calling. We must learn about the 5-fold ministries found in Ephesians 4 verse 11, understanding the unique way God has shaped us and what this means for our personal calling as a missional disciple.
- **The Hexagon** addresses the issue of prayer, especially the six phrases contained in the prayer that Jesus taught his disciples. Disciples must learn how to pray and we use the Lord's Prayer as the template that leads to a substantial relationship with the Father. In doing so, we also learn the importance of the Trinity and learn to appreciate the work of the Holy Spirit in our world, connecting us with the Father.
- **The Heptagon** concerns communal life and health. We learn how to identify the seven signs of healthy life and learn to live in, participate and contribute to the spiritual family of which we are a part.
- Finally, we consider Jesus' evangelistic strategy - Mission through 'People of Peace'. We learn to step out in bold mission by identifying 'People of Peace' and helping them live in the spiritual breakthrough God has prepared for them. We learn what the gospel is and a simple and clear articulation of it that can be shared with 'People of Peace'. This process is represented by **The Octagon** (eight keys to relational mission).

Each shape serves as a kind of entry point, with an endless number of Scripture passages, stories or practices attached. The biggest question isn't whether someone can teach for hours on a silly shape, but does his or her life actually embody and incarnate the 'shape' and Scripture teaching, and can this person multiply that into someone else's life? That was Jesus' criterion and so it must be ours as well.

As I have already quoted in Chapter 13, Andy Stanley lists five primary ways that people experience growth in their faith:

- Practical teaching
- Private disciplines
- Personal ministry
- Providential relationships
- Pivotal circumstances

In my opinion LifeShapes incorporate all these means of growth. (To find out more about LifeShapes, please refer to the resources section at the end of the book.)

Chapter 19: India, UK and Europe

India

In India, the general view is that a church consists of a building, a Sunday service and a minister. Planting or leading a church is seen as a means to make a living and personal prestige. Very often, it can be regarded as a kind of 'family business' that is to be passed on and kept within the family.

There has also been widespread teaching of the Prosperity Gospel and Dispensational Theology, whereas there has been little teaching of hermeneutics (rules governing the interpretation of Scripture) or principles of the Kingdom and therefore it is difficult to communicate the principles of discipleship as outlined in this work. In order to prepare the way for creating a multiplying discipleship movement we have found that a real paradigm shift is necessary, not least a real understanding of the Gospel of the Kingdom.

Having spent a lot of time with a few teachable young people, we have noticed that a change in the way of thinking has been slowly happening with the result that all have found a disciple and some of those disciples have already found someone to disciple themselves. Paul wrote to Timothy in 2 Timothy 2:2 saying, *"And the things you have heard me say in the presence of many witnesses entrust to reliable people who will also be qualified to teach others."* Here we see four generations: Paul to Timothy; Timothy to faithful men; faithful men to others. In some cases, we are seeing up to the fourth generation already in India and, hopefully, in time we may see a multiplying discipleship movement take off.

In a nation where religious persecution is very real, this approach to evangelism is well suited. It is well documented that there have been many violent attacks on Christians by militant Hindus resulting in horrific injuries, displacement of whole Christian communities and even, on many occasions, martyrdom which is rarely brought to justice.

UK and Europe

As Europe becomes more and more secular, with the exception of growing Muslim populations, it becomes increasingly more difficult to conduct mass evangelism initiatives. The evangelical and Pentecostal/charismatic churches in nations like Spain, France and Denmark remain relatively small and don't appear to be making much impact on the traditional churches, such as Catholic in the case of France and Spain, and Lutheran in the case of Denmark. For example, in France it is actually illegal to distribute tracts or to hold open air meetings. Amazingly, the government prides itself on the creation of a secular society (despite the fact that there are significant Roman Catholic and Muslim populations, not to mention more registered mediums than there are registered doctors). A one-to-one disciple-making approach is not only ideal in such a spiritual environment, but it is also effective.

In the UK, things are a little better, but the results are still not what one would like to see. Most of the national growth and increase in churches is attributed to the increased number and size of our African churches. However, this paints a rather distorted picture. We may like to speak in terms of re-verse missions (Africans now coming to the UK to bring the gospel) but in actual fact many African churches do poorly at reaching the indigenous British population since their cross-cultural communication is somewhat lacking. Many continue to hold their services in French, and their worship has a distinctly African flavour. This is great for reaching French-speaking people of African heritage, but less effective when it comes to English speakers.

In a multicultural society such as we find in UK and Europe, the one-to-one disciple making approach is again ideal and effective. Our approach to UK and Europe whether it be toward Muslims, Roman Catholics or secularist sceptics, as I see it, must have the following six attributes:

1. It must demonstrate the love and compassion of Christ.
2. It must be grounded in lots of prayer.
3. It will depend on people discovering God in the Bible for themselves and obeying His Word.
4. It must be produce disciples who make disciples and churches that plant churches.

5. It will be achieved by ordinary people participating in an extraordinary harvest.
6. It must expect the miraculous favour of God to reproduce transformed people who are transforming whole societies.

Chapter 20: Final Exhortations

"In times of drastic change, it is the learners who inherit the future. The learned find themselves well-equipped to live in a world that no longer exists."

Eric Hoffer

The church now lives in a different world - a post-Christian world. We have to think in terms of making disciples in the same way that the early church did. As the number of people with a Christian/Bible background decreases, discipleship looks very different to what was accepted practice just a few years ago. If, for example, there are 10% of a population with some kind of church/faith background, it means that there is 90% without it. Thus, it makes sense to think in terms of churches cooperating to target the 90% rather than churches competing with one another for a 'market share' of the 10% (which flies in the face of Jesus' high priestly prayer that we should be one just as he and the Father are one).

The Church that Jesus is building is a grassroots people movement which is a bottom-up movement involving ordinary people with little structure. It is missional in that this church sees itself as the primary means to bring the gospel of the Kingdom to the world. It is a movement insomuch as it has a fluid structure and is a social force traveling like a virus from one person to another, with a leadership which leads from the front by modelling the desired qualities.

This can be illustrated in the form of an equation:

Multiplication church planting + Mission of all people everywhere = Apostolic Movement.

In the church that Jesus is building, conversion is commission. Another way of saying it is, baptism is ordination. Take your pick!

If we want to become an apostolic movement again, we must allow God's Spirit to play a leading role. He brings creativity, life and inspirational courage. We must ask ourselves hard questions about the extent to which we have replaced the leading of the Spirit with technique, ideology and top-heavy thinking in the life of the church. It is not so much that the church has a mission, it's more a case that mission has a church. Church follows mission, not the other way round!

Slogans in such a church might look like this:

- Every believer a disciple; every disciple a disciple-maker.
- Every believer a church planter; every church a church planting church.
- We don't go to church, we are the church!
- Your mission is your life!
- Discipleship is key!

In a world that is based on consumerism and instant results, and where success is defined by numbers, Jesus' disciple-making strategy is counterintuitive.

When we look at Jesus' approach the principles appear to be:

- Go slow at first in order to go faster later (or, as the saying goes, 'Do you want it done fast, or do you want it done right?');
- Focus on a few to win many;
- Engage an entire family or group through the individual;
- Share only when and where people are ready to hear;
- It's about discovering and obeying, not teaching and knowledge;
- Disciple people to conversion, not vice versa;
- Coach lost people from the beginning to discover and obey biblical truth;
- In many cases start with creation, not with Christ (especially with Muslims and other world religions);
- Prepare to spend a long time making strong disciples, but anticipate miraculous interventions that will accelerate the process;
- Expect the hardest places to yield the greatest results – often the most hostile communities can yield to discipling more rapidly than communities that have experienced traditional churches in their midst and become immunised from them.

Finally, by way of conclusion, a good definition of discipleship to leave you with might look like this:

'Discipleship is the process by which we are becoming conformed to the image of Christ and growing in the faith until it is no longer we who live, but Christ is living through us. It is not about how much we know, but what we do with what we know. This faith is stretched by being involved in ministry, where we are exhorted by teachers and leaders. As disciples, we are becoming fruitful by connecting with God through prayer, the Scriptures and other disciplines. Discipleship involves put-ting ourselves on the frontline of the cause of Christ and being led by God into unique situations that challenge us at every level. It involves interacting with other Christians where we sharpen each other as iron against iron and it demands participation, not passivity. Like a midwife assisting with a childbirth, it is something that can be aided but not done for us. It takes a church, but only goes as far as the person who is willing to be a committed lifelong learner.'

Resources and Helpful Models

Discovery Bible Study (DBS)

I have spoken about this approach to making disciples in Chapter 16. I recommend the book "Miraculous Movements: How Hundreds of Thousands of Muslims are Falling in Love with Jesus" by Jerry Trousdale.

Multiply Groups

I recommend this book, "Multiply: Disciples Making Disciples" by Francis Chan. It is an excellent book which can be used in the discipling process. There are 26 chapters and so, meeting weekly, it can be covered in six months. It covers the areas of living as a disciple maker, living as the church, how to study the Bible, understanding the Old Testament, understanding the New Testament, and a section on the question of "Where Do We Go from Here?"

Life Transformation Groups (LTGs)

I have spoken about this approach to making disciples in Chapter 17. I recommend the book "Search & Rescue" by Neil Cole. I also mentioned ABC Groups, which are based on the Discovery Groups espoused by Floyd McClung in his book "Follow: A Simple and Profound Call to Live Like Jesus".

LifeShapes (Mike Breen - 3DM)

I have spoken about this approach to making disciples in Chapter 18. I recommend the book "Building a Discipling Culture" by Mike Breen. There are many resources surrounding this approach which may be obtained through 3DM.

The Alpha Course (Nicky Gumbel - Alpha)

This course is known world-wide and, as such, needs no comment. It is ideal for bringing those with some Christian/Church background through to becoming a disciple.

Acknowledgements

Recommended books that I have borrowed heavily from throughout this work:

'Rediscovering the Kingdom of God' by Myles Munroe (Destiny Image Publishers)

'From Eternity to Here' by Frank Viola (David C Cook)

'Crazy Love' by Francis Chan (David C Cook)

'Radical' by David Platt (Multnomah Books)

'On the Verge: A Journey into the Apostolic Future of the Church' by Alan Hirsch and Dave Ferguson (Exponential Series)

Other Recommended Books:

'Simple Ways to Reach Out to Muslims' by Carl Medearis (Bethany House E-Book)

'Simply Jesus' by N.T. Wright (HarperCollins)

'Surprised by Hope' by N.T. Wright (SPCK Publishing)